Bach Among the Theologians

JAROSLAV PELIKAN

Bach Among the Theologians

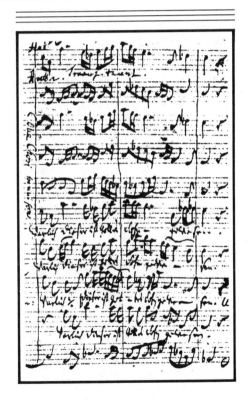

FORTRESS PRESS   PHILADELPHIA

Library of Congress Cataloging-in-Publication Data

Pelikan, Jaroslav Jan, 1923–
  Bach among the theologians.

  Includes bibliographical references and index.
  1. Bach, Johann Sebastian, 1685–1750—Criticism and interpretation. 2. Bach, Johann Sebastian, 1685–1750—Religion. 3. Theology, Lutheran. I. Title.
ML410.B1P37 1986   230'.41'0924   86-7609
ISBN 0-8006-0792-9

1711C86   Printed in the United States of America   1-792

To Joseph Sittler,
for what he has taught me
about all five Evangelists

Contents

Preface

Bach Among the Theologians is the product of visits by a historical theologian among the Bach scholars. In 1950, for the commemoration of the two-hundredth anniversary of the death of Johann Sebastian Bach, I undertook some studies and delivered some lectures that eventually became the sixth and final chapter of my little book, *Fools for Christ*, published in 1955 by Muhlenberg Press, the predecessor of Fortress Press. Sensing (correctly) that this was my favorite among the chapters of that book, various readers— including especially Joseph Sittler, who had heard the original— urged me to expand it into a full-length consideration of Bach in the context of the theology of his time. As opportunity arose in the succeeding decades, I kept on returning to this idea: analyzing chorale texts, comparing homiletical and musical treatments of various biblical passages, reading the other writings of Bach's librettists, scribbling memoranda to myself on concert programs and church bulletins, and picking the brains of musicians professional and amateur, including the one with whom I share my life.

The three-hundredth anniversary of Bach's birth in 1985 seemed to be the appropriate time, and invitations from various institutions for the anniversary seemed to provide the proper occasion, for finally undertaking a systematic study of the relations between Bach and the theology of the first half of the eighteenth century. Among those many hosts, let me mention at least three: the Aston Magna Academy, Boston University, and the Cyril Richardson Lecture at Union Theological Seminary. The generosity of J. Irwin

Miller and Xenia Miller gave me the scholarly leisure I needed for my research, and the William Clyde DeVane Lectureship at Yale provided me with the audience for pulling all of this together.

My spiritual, aesthetic, and intellectual life has been enriched by the opportunity to have a part in a great many public presentations of Bach's sacred music during 1985, and my interpretations have benefited from the host of experts on Bach who have shared their insights with me in response to my lectures: in my Yale audiences, my musical colleagues (in alphabetical order) Ward Davenny, Richard French, Fenno Heath, Charles Krigbaum, Thomas Murray, and Kerala Snyder, together with my teaching assistant/organists, David Connell and Gregory Peterson; Z. Philip Ambrose, who generously made available to me his edition and translation of the church cantatas before its publication; in a class by herself (in this respect as in most others), Rosalyn Tureck; two other performers of Bach's instrumental music, Paul Manz and Daniel Stepner, for their critical judgments on aspects of Bach's sacred music; two musicologists, Robert Marshall and particularly Christoph Wolff, from whose published works and personal comments I learned much of what appears in this book; and two conductors who have become my friends, Robert Shaw and Richard Westenburg, each of whom put on an unforgettable performance of the *Saint Matthew Passion* "back to back" with my lectures. Having thanked that distinguished company, I probably have more reason than most to observe the authorial convention of adding that all the mistakes in this book remain my own.

For while this book is the product of my visits among Bach scholars, it is, quite obviously, anything but an invasion of their territory. As a historian of the development of Christian doctrine, I have taken a greater scholarly interest than many of my predecessors in its liturgical and biblical context. Having now come, in my work on the fifth and final volume of *The Christian Tradition*, to the period of Bach, I have, here in *Bach Among the Theologians*, employed the texts of his sacred music as a case study in the methodological problem of how to handle the liturgical and biblical setting of Christian thought. My underlying conviction is that both the Christian tradition and the music of Bach can be understood better through such scholarly investigation.

Most of the texts with which I have dealt were originally written in German. For the Lutheran chorales, I have made it a practice to use existing translations from various hymnals; for the cantatas, I have quoted the English translations of Z. Philip Ambrose; for the *Passions*, I have drawn upon several English translations coming out of program notes for concerts and record albums, without pedantically indicating which I have used where; for the text of the Bible itself, I have usually quoted the Revised Standard Version, except where the sense of Bach's (and Luther's) German version seemed to make the Authorized Version preferable. In all those quotations I have tried to retain whatever conventions for the capitalization of nouns and pronouns referring to the Deity had been observed in each of those sources.

The dedication is the expression of gratitude for a personal and scholarly association going back more than forty years.

Abbreviations

Ambrose, Cantatas	Z. Philip Ambrose, ed. and trans. *The Texts to Johann Sebastian Bach's Church Cantatas.* Neuhausen and Stuttgart, 1984
ANF	*The Ante-Nicene Fathers of the Church.* 10 vols. Grand Rapids, Mich.: Zondervan Publishing House, 1956
Arnold, *Bach*	Denis Arnold. *Bach.* Past Masters. New York: Oxford University Press, 1984
BJb	*Bach-Jahrbuch.* 1904ff.
BWV	Wolfgang Schmieder. *Thematisch-systematisches Verzeichnis der musikalischen Werke von Johann Sebastian Bach. Bach-Werke-Verzeichnis.* Leipzig, 1950
David-Mendel, *Bach Reader*	Hans T. David and Arthur Mendel, eds. *The Bach Reader: A Life of Johann Sebastian Bach in Letters and Documents.* Rev. ed. New York: W. W. Norton & Co., 1966
Julian, *Dictionary*	John Julian. *A Dictionary of Hymnology.* 2d rev. ed. 2 vols. New York: Dover Publications, 1957
Köchel	Hellmuth von Hase, ed. *Der kleine Köchel. Chronologisches und systematisches Verzeichnis sämtlicher musikalischer Werke von Wolfgang Amadeus Mozart.* Wiesbaden: Breitkopf und Härtel, 1961
LBW	*Lutheran Book of Worship*

LTK	*Lexikon für Theologie und Kirche.* 2d ed. 10 vols. and index. Freiburg, 1957–67
LW	Jaroslav Pelikan and Helmut T. Lehmann, eds. *Luther's Works: American Edition.* 55 vols. St. Louis: Concordia Publishing House, and Philadelphia: Fortress Press, 1955–86
Marshall, Process	Robert Lewis Marshall. *The Compositional Process of J. S. Bach: A Study of the Autograph Scores of the Vocal Works.* Vol. 1. Princeton: Princeton University Press, 1972
New Grove	*The New Grove Dictionary of Music and Musicians.* Edited by Stanley Sadie. New York: Macmillan Co., 1980
NPNF	*Nicene and Post-Nicene Fathers of the Church.* First and Second Series. Grand Rapids, Mich.: Zondervan Publishing House, 1979
Petzoldt, Ausleger	Martin Petzoldt, ed. *Bach als Ausleger der Bibel.* Göttingen, 1985
PRE	*Realenzyklopädie für protestantische Theologie und Kirche.* 3d ed. 22 vols. and index. Leipzig, 1896–1909
Schweitzer, Bach	Albert Schweitzer. *J. S. Bach.* Translated by Ernest Newman. 2 vols. New York: Macmillan Co., 1966
Smend, Bach-Studien	Friedrich Smend. *Bach-Studien: Gesammelte Reden und Aufsätze.* Edited by Christoph Wolff. Kassell, 1969
Spitta, Bach	Philipp Spitta. *Johann Sebastian Bach: His Work and Influence on the Music of Germany, 1685–1750.* Translated by Clara Bell and J. A. Fuller-Maitland. 3 vols. New York: Dover Publications, 1951
Szeskus, Aufklärung	Reinhard Szeskus, ed. *Johann Sebastian Bach und die Aufklärung.* Leipzig, 1982
TLH	*The Lutheran Hymnal*
Wolff, Bach Family	Christoph Wolff and others. *The New Grove Bach Family.* New York: W. W. Norton & Co., 1983

INTRODUCTION

1

The Four Seasons of J. S. Bach

In 1725, Bach's Venetian contemporary Antonio Vivaldi—who was born seven years earlier than Bach, in 1678, and died nine years earlier than Bach, in 1741—published, in Amsterdam, a concerto bearing the title *The Test of Harmony and Invention [Il cimento dell'armonia e dell'invenzione]*, numbered as opus 8 in the standard catalogue of Vivaldi's works. The first four parts of that concerto bear the subtitle *The Four Seasons [Le quatro stagioni]* and are certainly the best known of Vivaldi's works, having been recorded literally dozens of times. The idea of a musical composition inspired by Spring, Summer, Autumn, and Winter is not unique to Vivaldi (though he may have been the first to treat it in purely instrumental fashion); for example, Jean Baptiste Lully had composed a ballet on the same subject as early as 1661, and other composers, including both Haydn and Tchaikovsky, wrote works under this title as well. But Vivaldi has come to be so closely identified with it that upon hearing the simple title *The Four Seasons* without a specified composer most listeners will automatically think of him.

Vivalid was one of the few "composers of his own generation . . . to whom [Bach] was deeply indebted."[1] Indeed, it has been said that "his confrontation with Vivaldi's music in 1713-14 provoked what was certainly the strongest single development towards Bach's personal style," whose "unmistakable identity came about through his coupling of Italianisms with complex counterpoint, marked by busy interweavings of the inner voices as well as harmonic refinement."[2] As Hans-Günter Klein has shown, Vivaldi's significance for

Bach's compositional style extends far beyond his transcriptions of the Venetian master's string works for keyboard instruments.[3] But these transcriptions do not include *The Four Seasons*, and there is no known work of Bach bearing that title.

In speaking here of "the four seasons of J. S. Bach," therefore, it is not the four seasons of the climate but the four seasons of the church year—as set by the four major festivals of Christmas and Epiphany (including Advent), Easter (including Lent), Pentecost (including Ascension Day), and Trinity Sunday (including the "ferial" or "nonfestive" cycle of the Sundays after Trinity)—that are decisive. For these seasons determined the rhythm of Bach's musical activity and set the program for his works as both composer and performer. What has recently been said of the medieval *Corpus Christi Plays* would apply no less to Bach's music: "The liturgical year is the context in which the church commemorates, day by day, all history."[4] The structure of the church year as Bach inherited it had been evolving since the beginnings of Christianity. Indeed, controversy over its observance, and particularly over the proper date for the celebration of Easter (whether it should always be on the fourteenth day of Nisan according to the Jewish calendar or always on a Sunday), had broken out already in the second century.[5] At the first ecumenical council of the church, the Council of Nicea in 325, the date of Easter was, alongside the question of the relation between the Father and the Son in the Trinity, a major item on the agenda.[6] And until the Synod of Whitby in 664 the difference between the Roman and the Celtic system for Easter dominated the debates within the English church.[7] There were no similar conflicts in the early centuries over the dates of the other two major festivals: Pentecost always came fifty days after Easter, whatever the date of Easter might be; and Christmas was a relatively late addition to the Christian year.[8] An even later addition was Trinity Sunday, which was a medieval invention. Trinity Sunday was unusual among the festivals of the church year also because it did not observe an event but a doctrine.[9] Except for the abolition of such festivals as Corpus Christi as well as of some saints' days and Marian festivals, the Lutheran and Anglican Reformations (by contrast with Calvinism and especially Puritanism) had left the fundamental outline of the church year intact, and in Bach's time the churches he served continued to observe it. That becomes evident, for example, in the call he received to Halle on 14 December 1713 (which in the end he did not accept); it specified his duties for "all high holidays and feast days, and any others as they occur."[10]

1. Commemoration of Advent and Christmas, as the opening of the liturgical year, provided an opportunity for a consideration of the church year as a whole. Erdmann Neumeister (1671–1756), Lutheran pastor in Hamburg, who wrote the texts for several of Bach's cantatas, was the author of a book entitled *Christian Instruction on the God-pleasing Observance of Advent, Christmas, and New Year's*. The opening of a new church year, he admonished, should be the occasion for gratitude "that a merciful God has once again, for an entire year, preserved his holy word and holy sacraments for us, pure and unalloyed." It should, furthermore, provide an opportunity for reflection on the question, "How have we made use of this grace?" and, if the answer to the question was an admission of negligence (as it ought to be), for a repentant plea that God would forgive such negligence. Finally, the opening of the new church year was the appropriate time "to pray devoutly that [God] would continue to grant us this grace and to preserve his precious word and sacraments for us and for our posterity."[11] Citing the precedent of church councils from the early Middle Ages, Neumeister explained that Advent, like Lent, was a penitential season, during which, for example, there were to be no weddings.[12] The threefold advent of Christ—in the flesh at his birth, in the means of grace through word and sacrament, and in judgment at the end of time—provided the topics for the Scripture readings and sermons on three Sundays of the Advent season.[13]

None of this was particularly original with Neumeister, of course; and, for that matter, as an orthodox theologian he would not have wanted to lay claim to originality. But he did formulate it in a way that helps us to understand Bach's music for Advent and Christmas. Thus Neumeister's comments on traditional church practice explain why it was that in 1723, Bach's first year at Leipzig, "from the second Sunday in Advent to the fourth, came his first break in the weekly routine of composing and performing cantatas"; for "in Leipzig, unlike Weimar, this period was a 'tempus clausum,' as was Lent up to and including Palm Sunday."[14] Likewise, Neumeister's enumeration of the several comings of Christ had already been outlined, for example, in the Hussite hymn

"Gottes Sohn ist kommen," by Luther's contemporary, Jan Roh, bishop of the Unity of Bohemian Brethren:[15]

> Once he came in blessing,
> All our ills redressing . . . .
>
> Still he comes within us;
> Still his voice would win us . . . .
>
> Come, then, O Lord Jesus,
> From our sins release us;
> Let us here confess you,
> Till in heav'n we bless you.

Roh's hymn had been included (though usually under the name Horn, which is the German translation of the Czech name Roh) in various German Lutheran hymnals during the period between his own time and Bach's. "Gottes Sohn ist kommen" became, in turn, the basis for one of the chorale preludes (*BWV* 703) in Bach's *Clavier-Übung*, a fughetta ascribed to the years 1739–42.

Neumeister defined *Weihnachten*, Christmas, as "a holy night, because on [this night] the all-holy Son of God was born into this world as a human child"; for, he explained, the word *weihen* in *Weihnachten*, "to consecrate," meant "the same as 'to make holy,' and 'to be consecrated' as 'to be holy.' "[16] He took his explanation of Christmas as an occasion to denounce secular celebrations of Christmas Eve "by the children of darkness" as "abominable, superstitious, and ungodly."[17] The authentic celebration of the festival, by contrast, had the following components: attending divine worship; reflecting at home on the meaning of the word of God; pondering the grace of God; "rejoicing over thy birth and grace [*Geburt und Gnade*]"; thanking and praising God; and doing good to one's neighbor.[18] All those ways of celebrating Christmas resound throughout the six cantatas that comprise Bach's *Christmas Oratorio* (*BWV* 248). Instead of the simple alliteration "Geburt und Gnade [birth and grace]," the soprano arioso in Cantata IV of the *Christmas Oratorio* has the much more complex alliterative pattern (from W to H to Sch, and then back again):

> Jesu, meine Freud' und Wonne,
> Meine Hoffnung, Schatz und Teil,
> Mein Erlöser, Schutz und Heil,
> Hirt und König, Licht und Sonne!

Ach, wie soll ich *würdiglich*,
Mein *Herr* Jesu, preisen dich?

[Jesu, my joy and delight,
My hope, my treasure and my portion,
My redeemer, refuge and salvation,
My shepherd and king, my light and sun!
Oh, how shall I worthily
Praise thee, my Lord Jesus?]

But Neumeister's admonitions of reflection, joy, thanks, and responsibility to the neighbor are recurring ideas, here as well as in many other considerations of the proper way to observe "Weihnachten" as a "consecrated night."

(2. Because of the central importance of the *Passions* in the corpus of Bach's sacred music, the significance of the second of the "four seasons," the season of Lent and Easter, will concern us at great length in chapters 6 to 8.)

3. For our purposes, we may take the Feast of the Ascension and the Feast of Pentecost together as one "season." In fact, as recent studies have shown, the two were celebrated together on the fiftieth day after Easter, as late as the end of the fourth century.[19] Therefore the very name "Pentecost" in Greek (and in Tertullian's Latin) before that time refers not to the fiftieth day but to all fifty days.[20] Thus the church historian Eusebius, describing the death of the emperor Constantine (which had been immediately preceded by his baptism), recounts:

> All these events occurred during a most important festival, I mean the august and holy solemnity of Pentecost, which is distinguished by a period of seven weeks, and sealed with that one day on which the holy Scriptures attest the ascension of our common Saviour into heaven, and the descent of the Holy Spirit among men. In the course of this feast the emperor received the privileges I have described [above all, baptism]; and on this last day of all, which one might justly call the feast of feasts, he was removed about mid-day to the presence of his God.[21]

Pentecost, then, was not only "the feast of feasts," as Eusebius here calls it but an entire "season" of the church year as this was developing in the early church.

The somewhat ambiguous place of the Pentecost season in the church year and of the festival of Pentecost in the liturgy became an important factor when the doctrine of the Holy Spirit finally received the attention it deserved, in the final quarter of the fourth century. The primitive Christian practice of addressing hymns and prayers to the person of Jesus as divine, "Christo quasi Deo" (as the earliest pagan description of the Christian community says), had provided the defenders of the orthodox dogma of the Council of Nicea, that Christ the Son of God was "one in being with the Father," with an all but irrefutable argument; for their opponents, too, continued to use such hymns and prayers for Christ (as would the antitrinitarians of the Reformation era), despite their rejection of the dogma.[22] But when it came to clarifying the relation between the Holy Spirit and the Father rather than the Son and the Father, the opponents were able to ask, "Who in ancient or modern times ever worshipped the Spirit? Who ever prayed to Him? Where is it written that we ought to worship Him, or to pray to Him, and whence have you derived this tenet of yours?"[23] The best the orthodox could do in response was, first, to cite the baptismal formula, "in the name of the Father and of the Son *and of the Holy Spirit,*" and, second, to lay claim to an "unwritten tradition" in support of such worship.[24]

Whatever the validity of such claims and arguments may have been, the Western church, once the doctrine of the full deity of the Holy Spirit was promulgated, went on to repair the inadequacy by providing hymns and prayers addressed to the Third Person of the Trinity, "Spiritui quasi Deo." The most important of these were the several Latin hymns that opened with the word "Veni," in particular the "Veni, Creator Spiritus" (often attributed to Rabanus Maurus) and the "Veni, Sancte Spiritus" (usually attributed now to Stephen Langton). The first of these, as John Julian says, "has taken deeper hold of the Western Church than any other mediaeval hymn, the *Te Deum* alone excepted."[25] Of the more than fifty vernacular translations that Julian lists (and there are many others, in several languages), the first is "*Komm, Gott Schöpfer, heiliger Geist* . . . a full and faithful version by M. Luther, 1st pub. in *Eyn Enchiridion,* Erfurt, 1524." In addition, Luther adapted two other medieval hymns for Pentecost, producing "Nun bitten wir den heiligen Geist [To God the Holy Spirit let us pray]" (*LBW* 317) and "Komm Heiliger Geist, Herre Gott [Come, Holy Ghost, God and Lord]" (*LBW* 163).[26] Luther accused some of his left-wing opponents of claiming that they had "devoured the Holy Spirit feathers and all"; at the same time, he charged others with being "fine Easter preachers, but very poor Pentecost preachers," because they preached "solely about the redemption of Jesus Christ," but not about the "sanctification by the Holy Spirit."[27] His three Pentecost hymns, which are among his finest, were part of his effort, long overlooked by Reformation scholars, to accord to the Holy Spirit the proper place of honor in Christian theology, preaching, and worship.[28]

These hymns were to play a prominent part in Bach's music for the Pentecost season. "Komm, Gott Schöpfer, Heiliger Geist," Luther's version of "Veni, Creator Spiritus," is the basis of *BWV 370* and again of *BWV 631* and *BWV 667*; "Nun bitten wir den Heiligen Geist" of *BWV 385*; and "Komm, Heiliger Geist, Herre Gott" of what Albert Schweitzer calls "brilliant and animated," a "mystical chorale,"[29] the organ fantasia *BWV 651* and *BWV 652*. In addition, *BWV 671* and *BWV 674* in part 3 of the *Clavier-Übung* are chorale preludes on "Kyrie, Gott Heiliger Geist," and *BWV 295* on "Des heil'gen Geistes reiche Gnad'." On Thursday, 19 May 1735, the Feast of the Ascension, Bach conducted the first performance of what has come to be called his *Ascension Oratorio*, "Lobet Gott in seinen Reichen" (*BWV 11*),[30] by an unknown librettist, parts of which were recycled from a secular cantata, "Froher Tag, verlangte Stunden" (*BWV Anhang 18*), composed for the reopening of the renovated Thomasschule in Leipzig on 5 June 1732. The *Ascension Oratorio* was, in turn, to provide grist for the mill of the *Mass in B Minor* (*BWV 232*). The "Agnus Dei" of the *Mass*, adapted in 1747–49, near the end of Bach's life, comes from the alto aria of the *Ascension Oratorio*, "Ach bleibe doch, mein liebstes Leben"; but, as has been noted, "only one long phrase of it is used, and the remainder is quite a new composition."[31]

4. The fourth, and by far the longest, of "the four seasons of J. S. Bach" was the period beginning with Trinity Sunday and running until the last Sunday before Advent, thus for approximately half of the church year. As the old doggerel couplet has it,

> The sermons go on into infinity,
> To the twenty-sixth Sunday after Trinity.

In the medieval church calendar, the monotony of these six months had been broken up by a series of special feasts and festivals, beginning with the Feast of Corpus Christi, commemorated on the Thursday after Trinity Sunday, through the Feast of the Assumption of the Blessed Virgin Mary on 15 August, to the feasts of All Saints' Day and All Souls' Day on 1–2 November. There were also, of course, many individual saints' days in this season, including—by statistical average, as likely as not to fall into this period—the feast day of the patron saint of the village or parish. The Lutheran Reformation did not abolish all of these everywhere and at once. As we shall be noting at greater length in the next chapter, moreover, the Lutheran Church also provided some of its own replacements for these lost festivals: 25 June, the anniversary of the presentation of the Augsburg Confession in 1530; 31 October, for the day on which, in 1517, Luther had posted the Ninety-five Theses, which set off the Reformation; 10 November, Luther's birthday in 1483 (replacing St. Martin's Day, 11 November, on which Luther was baptized and from which he derived his Christian name); and often the anniversary of the introduction of the Reformation into a particular territory. Nevertheless, the nonfestive cycle of the church year could become quite dreary and didactic.

Whatever problems that may have posed for preacher and people, it presented a genuine challenge to the church musician, as Bach discovered when he moved to Leipzig on 22 May 1723 (although he had performed there earlier). Philipp Spitta has well summarized the situation:

> Bach had entered on his post in the ferial portion of the ecclesiastical year. Remarkable as was the activity displayed by him as a church composer during this period, yet he had no opportunity of showing himself in his full greatness until the beginning of the ecclesiastical year 1723–1724.[32]

We should perhaps add that there were also individual occasions, beginning almost immediately after his inauguration at Leipzig, for which Bach prepared special compositions. It is probably to one of these, a funeral service for Johanna Maria Kesse, widow of the postmaster of Leipzig, that we owe the motet "Jesu meine Freude" (BWV 227). But on the First Sunday after Trinity, 30 May 1723, Bach conducted the first of his Leipzig cantatas (BWV 75), "Die Elenden sollen essen [The hungering shall be nourished]" (Ambrose, Cantatas 191–94). The composition of these cantatas for the church year represented what Christoph Wolff has called "a musical enterprise without parallel in Leipzig's musical history: in a relatively short time he composed five complete cycles of cantatas for the church year, with about 60 cantatas in each, making a repertory of roughly 300 sacred cantatas."[33] Of these, about one-third have been lost. Those that remain stand as evidence, above all of course for Bach's individual genius but also for his vocation as a church musician and for the decisive function of the church year in providing the basic framework within which the vocation of this genius was to express itself. The significance of that vocation deserves consideration in its own right, as we shall have frequent occasion to note throughout this book and especially once again in its conclusion. For the interpretation of the cantatas and church music of Bach, such a definition of his vocation means that the context of his compositional activity was the liturgical year, as this usually indicated and frequently prescribed both the texts he was to use and the chorales upon which he was to draw. It suggests as well that the notion of patronage, which has proved to be so fruitful for research in art history, applies no less forcefully in the history of music. Michelangelo and Bach created what they did because they were commissioned to do so by popes and church councils, or by noblemen and town councils. As we shall see repeatedly, he likewise shared with other great figures of past and present an exasperating tendency to contradict himself and to change his mind, as experience—or, for that matter, expediency—suggested.

The recognition of the four seasons of the liturgical year as the context for Bach's work has at least one other methodological implication for the interpretation of his compositions: the role of historical research in the interpretation of his sacred music. One of the most distinguished leaders in such historical research and in the twentieth-century recovery of the music of the Baroque period on the basis of that research, the late Ralph Kirkpatrick, observed that "it has now become all too easy to regard certain perennial unanswered and unanswerable questions as already answered by the documents of history." "One cannot," he concluded with his characteristic dry wit, "sidestep artistic and interpretive problems by relegating them to the dictates of historical authority."[34] Precisely for that reason, however, so clear (and, in a majority of instances, "answerable") a question as the Sunday of the church year for which a particular piece of music was composed does constitute an important historical datum for addressing the "artistic and interpretive problems" associated with its full realization today. Thus Spitta speaks of "Bach's way of giving force and point to a tedious or digressive cantata text by seizing upon the emotional character of the Sunday or festival."[35] Even when audiences cannot be expected to understand the German, therefore, there is good reason to pay attention to the season in scheduling the music—particularly in a church but also in a concert hall or on the air. As we shall have frequent occasion to note, Bach did move melodies and texts from one season of the church year to another, but he did not do so inattentively, indiscriminately, or arbitrarily. Rather, the four seasons were parts of a single entity, the church year, each part of which was pertinent to the other parts. Echoes and reminders of one season, therefore, were appropriate to the music of another. Above all, the centrality of the story of the crucifixion and resurrection of Christ implied that "Lenten music" was always pertinent. Modern audiences may find the Lenten portions of *Messiah* disturbing to their thoughts about the birth of the baby Jesus, and modern conductors may feel justified in pandering to that sentimentality by excising those portions and thus transforming the oratorio into a Christmas cantata—and "Hallelujah" into a Christmas carol, when it is in fact a celebration of the victory of the resurrection of Christ.[36] But, as his texts seemed to require, Bach was not embarrassed to introduce the chorales of Lent into the music for all four seasons.

Not only were the four seasons of the church year the fundamental structure for most of Bach's work as a composer but time itself repeatedly provided the topic for it. The organ chorale "Das alte Jahr vergangen ist" (*BWV* 614) appears to come from Bach's Weimar period and has been dated by scholars at 1713/14. At Cöthen, where the established church was Reformed rather than Lutheran,[37] Bach was apparently expected to compose secular cantatas for New Year's Day. From one of these, for 1720, "Dich loben die lieblichen Strahlen" (*BWV* A6), we have only the text; but for the cantata from the preceding year (*BWV* 134a), "Die Zeit, die Tag und Jahre macht [The time that makes both days and years]," there are both words and music. But, symbolically if not also substantively, the most appropriate cantata to summarize the meaning of the "four seasons" for Bach was written early in 1708: the funeral cantata (*BWV* 106), "Gottes Zeit ist die allerbeste Zeit [God's own time is the very best of times]" (Ambrose, *Cantatas* 266–67), whose prelude is often performed as a separate piece.[38] Spitta has devoted a careful and detailed, if sometimes a bit overwrought, analysis to this cantata, which in his judgment "has a depth and intensity of expression which reach the extreme limits of possibility of representation by music."[39] Schweitzer speaks of "the dramatic life and the intimate union of words and music" in this funeral cantata and says of it that "the text is as perfect as the music," suggesting that "Bach probably compiled the text of this cantata himself" from various sources.[40] We shall be returning to "Gottes Zeit" later, but for our present purposes it stands, in both text and music, as a reminder not only of the preoccupation with death (to be discussed in chapter 5) that was to produce "Komm, süsser Tod, komm, sel'ge Ruh" (*BWV* 478), for which Bach himself wrote the melody, but of the preoccupation with time and transiency, as this had been sacralized by the four seasons of the Christian year.

Part I

THE THEOLOGICAL CONTEXT OF BACH'S CHURCH MUSIC

2

The Musical Heritage
of the Reformation

The 25th of June 1730 was a red-letter day on the church calendar in many lands, for it was the two hundredth anniversary of the most important official document of the Reformation, the Augsburg Confession. For example, Bach's contemporary, the well-known preacher and theologian Valentin Ernst Loescher (1673–1749), spoke of "the year of jubilee 1730" and interpreted the actions of the Lutheran Salzburg émigrés in that year as "an honor that God has paid to the Augsburg Confession and to our jubilee celebration."[1] And another contemporary, Sigmund Jacob Baumgarten (1706–57), who has been called *"de facto* the one who made the transition from Pietism to Rationalism, at least for Halle,"[2] delivered a sermon on 25 June 1730 with the title "The Rescue of the Value and Sublimity of the Word of God through our Evangelical Confessors of the Faith"; as Baumgarten noted, that date had been "wisely designated by those in high office for the present jubilee service as a public observance of this blessing."[3]

The presentation of a confession of faith by the Protestant princes and free cities to the diet of the Holy Roman Empire held at the city of Augsburg, on 25 June 1530, had represented the coming of age of the Reformation, both politically and doctrinally. For if Luther's defiant words at Worms in 1521, "Here I stand. I cannot do otherwise!" were its Declaration of Independence, the Augsburg Confession was its Constitution. Therefore by Bach's time, the commemoration of its anniversary on 25 June had become, particularly in portions of southern Germany, a part of the Protestant church year. The centenary of the Augsburg Confession in 1630 had taken place during the Thirty Years' War and hence could not be observed properly. This was all the more reason that when it came time for the bicentenary, on 25 June 1730, it seemed particularly appropriate to mark the jubilee with special celebrations. As is well known, the tercentenary of the Augsburg Confession yet another hundred years later, on 25 June 1830, was to provide the occasion for Felix Mendelssohn-Bartholdy to compose his *Fifth Symphony* in D major, the "Reformation Symphony," whose fourth movement is a fugue-like elaboration of Luther's chorale, "Ein' feste Burg ist unser Gott." The composition of the *Fifth Symphony* falls into the very period of Mendelssohn's conscious engagement with the church music of Bach, leading up to the revival of the Bach *Passion according to Saint Matthew* on 11 March 1829, with, among others, Hegel in the audience.[4] In Leipzig, Johann Sebastian Bach marked the bicentenary of the Augsburg Confession by not one but three church cantatas, performed on three successive days, 25, 26, and 27 June: *BWV* 190a, "Singet dem Herrn ein neues Lied!" on the 25th; *BWV* 120b, "Gott, man lobet dich in der Stille" on the 26th; and *BWV* A4a, "Wünschet Jerusalem Glück" on the 27th. Unfortunately the music for all three of these cantatas has been lost, although we do have some of the texts, as well as some of the earlier music that Bach adapted for these works.

But that does not mean at all that we are bereft of musical documentation for Bach's celebration of the musical heritage of the Reformation. The chorales listed in the catalogue as *BWV* 302 and 303 are both settings of "Ein' feste Burg." Above all, there is the cantata (*BWV* 80) "Ein' feste Burg [A mighty fortress is our God]" (Ambrose, *Cantatas* 205–8), which was composed for the festival of the Reformation on the basis of a libretto by Salomo Franck, poet at the court of Weimar. "There is no certainty regarding [the present text] of the Reformation cantata, 'Ein' feste Burg,' "[5] which evidently is the result of a considerable evolution. Its earliest stages can be traced to Bach's stay in Weimar, where it seems originally to have been intended for presentation on the Third Sunday in Lent. It received greater elaboration with the addition of its stirring first movement and defiant fifth movement, when Bach revised it as a Reformation cantata in Leipzig. There is, moreover, a problem with the version of it found in the surviving manuscript copies, none of them in Bach's own hand, but one of them in the hand of his pupil and son-in-law, Johann Christoph Altnikol. The scoring it acquired when it was arranged by its nineteenth-century editor, Wilhelm Rust (1822–92)—for orchestral forces much more imposing than those which Bach himself had had at his disposal—shaped much of its performance until relatively modern times, when scholars of the Baroque period and conductors have worked together to recover what was taken to be Bach's own final version.

Cantata 80, "Ein' feste Burg," should be studied together with its companion piece (*BWV 79*), "Gott der Herr ist Sonn und Schild [God the Lord is sun and shield]" (Ambrose, *Cantatas* 203–5), which had been composed for Reformation Day, 31 October 1725. Both cantatas employ what has come to be called "the 'tumult' motive," by which Bach portrays "the tumult of combat, as if he desired to suggest to the hearer the hoof-beats of the horses and the rumbling of the marching columns."[6] There is likewise a parallel between its treatment of that " 'tumult' motive" in the words sung by soprano and bass,

> Gott, ach Gott, verlasz die deinen nimmermehr!
>
> [God, O God, forsake thy people
> Nevermore!]

and the aria setting in Cantata 80 of the familiar words from Luther's chorale,

> Mit unser Macht ist nichts getan,
> Wir sind gar bald verloren.
>
> [No strength of ours can match his might!
> We would be lost, rejected.]

Although there is no librettist specified in the editions of Cantata 79, it is interesting to note that Erdmann Neumeister chose those words of Ps. 84:11, "Gott der Herr ist Sonn und Schild," as the epigraph for his book *Spiritual Sacrifice of Incense [Geistliches Räuch-Opfer]*, published in 1751, the year after Bach's death.

In his analysis of Cantata 80, Philipp Spitta has paid special attention to the first and fifth parts, two of the three choral settings of "Ein' feste Burg" in the cantata (the second of Luther's four stanzas is given over to the aria duet for soprano and bass). In the fifth part, verse three of the chorale, whose text begins,

> Und wenn die Welt voll Teufel wär
> Und wollten uns verschlingen . . . .
>
> [Though hordes of devils fill the land
> All threat'ning to devour us . . . .] (*LBW* 228),

Spitta says, "The orchestra plays a whirl of grotesque and wildly leaping figures, through which the chorus makes its way undistracted and never misled . . . , as grandiose and characteristic as it is possible to conceive." Spitta advances the thesis that "the bold spirit of native vigour which called the German Reformation into being, and which still stirred and moved in Bach's art, has never found any artistic expression which could even remotely compare with this stupendous creation."[7]

For an understanding of Bach's relation to the musical heritage of the Reformation, it is essential to ask: Even allowing for his characteristic Romantic extravangances, is Spitta correct in speaking about "the bold spirit of native vigour which called the German Reformation into being" as a spirit that "still stirred and moved in Bach's art," not only in the "stupendous creation" of Cantata 80 but throughout Bach's sacred music? To be satisfying, a scholarly answer to that question must consider at least two closely inter-related issues: first and foremost, in Spitta's words, "Bach's art" and its dedication to the Reformation heritage; and second, though much more briefly, also in Spitta's words, "the bold spirit of native vigour which called the German Reformation into being" as that spirit had expressed itself in music. These two issues should be taken up in turn. In doing so, we need to be reminded of the axiom, formulated by Wilhelm Dilthey, that the true significance of Luther and his Reformation "cannot be fully appreciated merely on the basis of works of dogmatics. Its documents are the writings of Luther, the church chorale, the sacred music of Bach and Handel, and the structure of community life in the church."[8]

If some calamity, natural or man-made, were to obliterate the extant hymns of Martin Luther—which the catalogue of his works lists as thirty-eight in number[9]—as their German texts have been critically edited in volume 35 of the Weimar edition of *Luthers Werke* and as they are contained in English translation in volume 53 of the American Edition of *Luther's Works*, it would be largely, though not quite completely, possible to reconstruct all of the most important ones, both their words and their music, on the basis of the compositions of Johann Sebastian Bach (although some of the melodies would be considerably more elaborate than Luther's originals). We shall be turning to Luther's hymns, and to Bach's reworkings of Luther's hymns, throughout this book, especially to his hymns for Easter as we consider the *Passions* of Bach; for reasons that we shall have to take up later, Luther did not write any hymn that can truly be called Lenten, but he did compose hymns for both Christmas and Easter, as well as the Pentecost hymns to which we have already referred.

Since Luther's own time there has been scholarly—and, to be sure, sometimes not so scholarly—controversy about his achievements as a hymnographer. As Théodore Gérold has said,

> Martin Luther has rightly been called the Father of Protestant music in Germany. Thanks to his fundamentally religious mind, combined with genuine artistic feeling, as well as to his energy and determination, he succeeded in laying the foundations of a type of music which not only became an essential element in the Protestant religion, but exerted a beneficial influence upon the whole civilized world.

But Gérold goes on to summarize the present state of research:

> The question whether Luther himself composed the melodies of certain hymns, of which he had written the texts, has often been discussed. He was long believed to be the composer of most of the melodies of his chorales. Then, little by little, doubts arose and for a time no melodies at all were attributed to him. Recent research has made it possible to answer the question more accurately, and there is a fairly general agreement in attributing the melodies of four or five hymns to him.[10]

The early tendency was also to give Luther credit for the texts of many of the German hymns and spiritual songs of the sixteenth century that do not bear anyone else's name. For example, Neumeister discusses at some length the question of whether or not to attribute to Luther the sixteenth-century hymn about the Reformation,

> O Herre Gott, dein göttlich Wort
> Ist lang verdunkelt blieben.

[O God, our Lord, Thy holy Word
Was long a hidden treasure
Till to its place It was by grace
Restored in fullest measure.] (*TLH* 266)

—restored, of course, by the work of Luther and the Reformation. Neumeister concludes, quite correctly, that Luther himself did not write this hymn, and he suggests that it might have come from one of Luther's collaborators, perhaps Paul Speratus or Nicholas Selneccer.[11] In what appears to be its most recent publication in English, the hymn is labeled "Author unknown, 1527."[12]

On the other hand, it became customary earlier in this century, and not only for Luther's Roman Catholic detractors, to belittle his place in the history of church music, to dismiss him as little more than an amateurish tunesmith in his hymns and a somewhat bungling dilettante in his liturgies. In part, this confusion about Luther's place in the history of Christian hymnody is probably due to his habit of adopting and adapting ancient and medieval hymns, translating them from Latin into German or modernizing the German as the needs of his congregations required. As has been mentioned earlier, all three of his Pentecost hymns were in fact such adaptations.[13] So, for example, is also his hymn about Holy Communion, "Gott sei gelobet und gebenedeiet,"

Gott sei gelobet and gebenedeiet,
Der uns selber hat gespeiset
Mit seinem Fleische und mit seinem Blute,
Das gib uns Herr Gott, zu gute,
Kyrieleison.
Herr, durch deinen heiligen Leichnam,
Der von deiner Mutter Maria kam,
Und has heilige Blut
Hilf uns, Herr, aus aller Noth.
Kyrieleison.

[O Lord, we praise you, bless you, and adore you,
In thanksgiving bow before you.
Here with your body and your blood you nourish
Our weak souls that they may flourish.
O Lord, have mercy!
May your body, Lord, born of Mary,
That our sins and sorrows did carry,
And your blood for us plead
In all trial, fear, and need:
O Lord, have mercy!] (*LBW* 215)

To the consternation of other branches of Protestantism, Luther here quite unabashedly took this medieval eucharistic hymn, which identified the "body and blood of Christ" in the Lord's Supper with the body and blood born of Mary, calling it indeed the body of God, and he made it his own by adding additional stanzas. There is no reason to believe, from the setting of this hymn by Bach (*BWV* 322), that it created any similar consternation for him at all.

Thus it was entirely fitting when Bach's *Saint John Passion*,[14] commenting on the words of Jesus to Peter after the incident with the sword in the Garden of Gethsemane, "Shall I not drink the cup which the Father has given me?" (John 18:11), has the chorus sing a stanza from Luther's setting of the Lord's Prayer, "Vater unser im Himmelreich":

> [Thy will, O Lord, our God, be done
> On earth as round Thy heav'nly throne.
> Thy patience, Lord, on us bestow,
> That we obey in weal and woe.
> Stay Thou the hand and spoil the skill
> Of them that work against Thy will.] (*TLH* 458)

The same affirmation of the Reformation heritage is audible in Bach's other settings of Luther's hymns. A leading Swedish interpreter of that heritage in the twentieth century, Einar Billing, once summarized it in the proposition: Regard nothing as the theology of Luther that cannot be reduced to a simple corollary of the forgiveness of sins.[15] The proposition, which is fraught with all the dangers of oversimplification that attend such formulations, does nevertheless certainly hold as a way of reading Luther's hymns and spiritual songs, which articulate the principal components of his faith in the forgiveness of sins, and do so in a manner that effectively complements his biblical commentaries, sermons, and theological treatises. It holds as well for Bach's treatment of those hymns.

This is not the place for a full-length treatment of Luther's theology or of the "reformation of church and dogma" that took place during the four centuries between the deaths of Thomas Aquinas and Bonaventure in 1274 and the births of Bach and Handel in 1685. But for an understanding of the place of Bach in the development of Christian faith and doctrine and of his relation to the Reformation heritage, it will be helpful to rehearse at least some of the major emphases of what can fittingly be called Luther's christocentric existentialism, as these appear not only in Luther's theological works but in his hymns and liturgies. (Each of these three emphases was present, but in a significantly modified—or in this connection one should perhaps say "modulated"—form, both in Lutheran Orthodoxy and in the Pietism of Bach's time; and it will be the burden of later chapters to seek to disentangle the similarities and the differences between the Reformation and both Orthodoxy and Pietism on these issues.)

Luther's faith was rooted in a profound awareness of the crisis of the human predicament. In his own language he spoke of that awareness as *Anfechtung*. Quite appropriately, Bach built his cantata for the Sunday nearest Reformation Day in 1724, the Twenty-first Sunday after Trinity, 29 October 1724 (*BWV* 38), around the words and music that Luther wrote for his hymn version of Ps. 130 in 1523, "Aus tiefer Not schrei ich zu dir [In deep distress I cry to thee]" (Ambrose, *Cantatas* 110-12). Luther called Ps. 130 one of the "Pauline Psalms," along with Pss. 32, 51, and 143, because they dealt with so many of the topics of the epistles of Paul (who does indeed quote them) in their depiction of *Anfechtung* and the sense of sin;[16] and this hymn was sung by the congregation for Luther's burial on 20 February 1546:

> Out of the depths I cry to you;
> O Father, hear me calling.
> Incline your ear to my distress
> In spite of my rebelling.
> Do not regard my sinful deeds.
> Send me the grace my spirit needs;
> Without it I am nothing. (*LBW* 295)

As he could close the *Christmas Oratorio* with an overwhelming transposition into D major, complete with trumpets, of the familiar Lenten chorale "O Haupt voll Blut und Wunden [O bleeding head and wounded],"[17] so both in his Cantata 38 and in the two organ versions (*BWV* 686 and 687) of the chorale "Aus tiefer Not schrei' ich zu dir" in the *Clavier-Übung*, Bach exhibited how profoundly he had grasped the full scope of Luther's doctrine of sin, which transcended despair through faith, by unexpectedly introducing the musical language of joy into a chorale about *Anfechtung,* even though "there is apparently nothing in the text to justify this." It does not seem to strain the musical evidence to interpret this language of joy as Bach's articulation of Luther's "doctrine of repentance, according to which all true repentance leads of itself to the joyful certainty of salvation; and so the motive of joy, that struggles against the gloom of the music and eventually gains the upper hand, has a profound significance."[18]

That "motive of joy" in "the joyful certainty of salvation" had not come to Luther easily, but only after profound struggle, a struggle that continued to be necessary long after the certainty had been achieved. For, in Luther's classic phrase—which, it has been correctly said, "contains the whole of the theology of Luther"[19]—the believer was *simul justus et peccator,* "righteous and a sinner at the same time." Luther's hymns combined confession and celebration as they did because that duality of *simul justus et peccator* was ever present; Bach's appropriation of Luther's hymns preserved, and often even heightened, the counterpoint and contrast between confession and celebration. Although "Ein' feste Burg," both in Luther's original and in the several versions by Bach that have been enumerated earlier, would be an obvious example, a lesser-known hymn by Luther will serve at least as well instead: "Wär' Got nicht mit uns diese Zeit [Were God not with us all this time]," which served as the basis for the cantata bearing the same title (*BWV* 14), composed by Bach for the Fourth Sunday after Epiphany, 30 January 1735 (Ambrose, *Cantatas* 53–54). Like "Ein' feste Burg" and "Erhalt' uns, Herr," "Wär' Gott nicht mit uns diese Zeit" dealt with the Reformation. It employed the words of Ps. 124 to celebrate the rescue of the pure gospel of God from its enemies in church and state, as those words are sung in a fugue by Bach's chorus with an inversion of the units of the melody, while the melody line, the *cantus firmus,* is carried by the instruments:

> Wär' Gott nicht mit uns diese Zeit,
> So soll Israel sagen,
> Wär' Gott nicht mit uns diese Zeit,
> Wir hätten müssen verzagen.
>
> [Were God not with us all this time,
> Let Israel now say it:

> Were God not with us all this time,
> We would surely have lost courage.]

But then, in the aria,

> Gott, bei deinem starken Schützen
> Sind wir vor den Feinden frei,
>
> [God, through thine own strong protection
> Are we from our foes set free,]

the freedom that is God's gift, even amid the threats within and without, asserts itself, to the accompaniment of the woodwinds, as *simul justus et peccator,* weak by itself but mighty in the "strong protection [*starke Schützen*]" of God. The awareness that this cantata was composed and presented at Leipzig and in 1735, amid the tumultuous events of the War of the Polish Succession (in which August "the Strong," elector of Saxony, laid claim to the throne in Warsaw), only enhances its dramatic effectiveness.

Luther spoke about sin and about faith as he did because of the centrality of the person of Jesus Christ in his thought and experience. The historic doctrine of orthodox Christianity, that to achieve human salvation, God himself, the Second Person of the eternal Trinity, had become incarnate in the person of Jesus Christ, found in Luther one of its mightiest expositors of all time. He dealt with the doctrine of the incarnation in his biblical commentaries, finding it adumbrated throughout the Hebrew Bible; and he defended his understanding of it in his works of theological polemics, attacking both the Roman Catholic right for seeking to deal with a *Deus nudus,* God apart from the Incarnate One, and the Protestant left for having failed to grasp the full significance of the personal union of God and man in the one person of Jesus Christ. His sermons on the Gospels, of which we have more than a thousand, apply the incarnation as the key to the sayings and deeds of Jesus.[20]

Luther's mightiest affirmation of this doctrine in words and music was undoubtedly his versification of the Nicene Creed, which is usually called in German "Luthers groszer Glaube [Luther's great Credo]" but which he himself called "das deutsche Patrem." (The Nicene Creed was called "Patrem" rather than "Credo," because in the medieval church the priest would, more or less audibly, intone the opening words of the creed, "Credo in unum Deum," and then the choir, which everyone could hear, would pick it up with the following words, "Patrem omnipotentem.") In it he confessed the orthodox faith in the Trinity, and especially the traditional doctrine of the two natures in Christ, in language reminiscent of his Small Catechism of 1529. Bach's chorale prelude on this setting of the Creed (*BWV* 437), and above all his interpretation of it in the Catechism Preludes of the *Clavier-Übung* (*BWV* 680 and 681), manage by their sonority to convey the quality of Luther's faith in Christ. So, in remarkable fashion, does the closing choral setting of John 3:16 in the cantata (*BWV* 68) "Also hat Gott die Welt geliebt [In truth hath God the world so loved]" (Ambrose, *Cantatas* 174–75). But both the power and the tenderness of what this doctrine could mean may be sensed in a special way in Luther's Christmas hymns, and then in Bach's use of those hymns.

The best known of these, to church audiences and concert audiences alike, is Luther's poignant and simple Christmas song, "Vom Himmel hoch da komm' ich her [From heav'n above to earth I come]," in fifteen stanzas (*LBW* 51). The song was subtitled, apparently by Luther himself, "ein Kinderlied auf die Weihnacht [a Christmas carol for children]." It has the flavor of a folk song; its very first stanza, the words of the Christmas angel, employs phrases like "gute neue Mähr" and "singen und sagen," which were familiar from that tradition. There is a chorale prelude on it in Bach's *Orgel-Büchlein* (*BWV* 606), and there are two more settings in the *Clavier-Übung*: *BWV* 700, which is extremely early in its original version, being dated at 1708 or before; and *BWV* 701, which is perhaps heard more often. The most ambitious rendition of it was in the five "canonical variations" on it (*BWV* 769) that Bach prepared upon finally becoming a member of Lorenz Mizler's "Correspondirende Societät der Musicalischen Wissenschaften" in 1747.[21] In 1956, Igor Stravinsky, who urged that "Bach's cantatas . . . should be the centre of our repertoire,"[22] adapted this rendition for chorus and orchestra.[23] As Stravinsky's amanuensis and authoritative interpreter, Robert Craft, has put it,

Stravinsky's attitude strikes one as more respectful towards Bach than the dead hand of reverence. He reveals himself, making no claims in the name of Bach; and far from merging the two composers, the transcription of *Vom Himmel hoch* appears as a new manifestation and a new musical revelation of both. It is a revelation at the highest spiritual level music can reach.[24]

To be fully accurate, Craft should have spoken of *three* composers, for Bach was himself adapting Luther's hymn. But the adaptation of Luther's "Christmas carol for children" by Bach that is the most familiar, and to many tastes the most effective, occurs in the *Christmas Oratorio* (*BWV* 248). Although it is a unified work as it stands, this oratorio is in fact a collection of six cantatas, which were strung out over the six days on which Christmas was kept in 1734/35, the three days of Christmas, plus New Year's Day, the Sunday after New Year's, and Epiphany. (Conductors and choirs since Bach's day have repeatedly given thanks that in that particular year there were not, as there might have been, seven days of observance, since the Second Day of Christmas happened to have fallen on a Sunday in 1734.) Part One of the oratorio, composed to be sung on First Christmas Day, having begun with the summons,

> Jauchzet, frohlocket! auf, preiset die Tage!
>
> [Rejoice, be glad! up, praise thy days!]

concludes with a remarkable contrast: first the bass aria, whose stentorian tones and dramatic intervals express reverence and awe in the presence of the tremendous mystery:

> Grosser Herr und starker König,
> Liebster Heiland, o wie wenig
> Achtest du der Erden Pracht.
>
> [O great Lord, most mighty King,
> Most dear Saviour, o how lowly
> Dost thou deem earth's highest splendour.]

Then there follows the tenderest and most beloved of the stanzas of Luther's "children's carol," which has often been memorized by children for use as a bedtime prayer; it also finds an echo in the closing stanza of Phillips Brooks's carol "O Little Town of Bethlehem":

> Ach, mein herzliebes Jesulein!
> Mach' dir ein rein sanft Bettelein,
> Zu ruhn in meines Herzens Schrein,
> Dass ich nimmer vergesse dein.

[O dearest Jesus, holy child,
Prepare a bed, soft, undefiled,
A holy shrine, within my heart,
That you and I need never part.]

In that contrast between his settings of the "Grosser Herr und starker König" of the bass aria and of the "herzliebes Jesulein" of the chorale, Bach was affirming the totally objective and yet utterly subjective character of the faith in the Word made flesh, and thus making his own Luther's christocentric existentialism.

Not by Luther, yet completely in the spirit of that "christocentric existentialism," is Bach's motet "Jesu, meine Freude" (*BWV* 227), which seems to have been originally prepared for a funeral in July 1723, shortly after his arrival in Leipzig. It is based on a hymn text by Johann Franck, usually dated 1655, with the melody by Johann Crüger, composed a few years earlier:

Jesus, priceless treasure,
Source of purest pleasure,
Truest friend to me:
Ah, how long I've panted,
And my heart has fainted,
Thirsting, Lord, for thee!
Thine I am, O spotless Lamb;
I will suffer nought to hide thee,
Nought I ask beside thee. (*LBW* 457)

"Jesu, meine Freude" follows an almost geometrical pattern in the structure of its eleven movements, with the first and the last identical, the second and tenth echoing each other, and so on. But all this complex structure has as its uninterrupted theme, its theological *cantus firmus*, Luther's affirmation of the centrality of Jesus Christ as the beginning and the end of faith.

Johann Sebastian Bach's appropriation of the musical heritage of the Lutheran Reformation, however, consisted in more than simply his exploitation of so many of its chorales for his organ preludes, church cantatas, and *Passions*, central though that is to his oeuvre as a composer of sacred music. As Friedrich Smend has said, Bach's cantatas "are not intended to be works of music or art on their own, but to carry on, by their own means, the work of Luther, the preaching of the word and of nothing but the word."[25] For Bach's relation to the heritage of Luther's Reformation was, to borrow an Aristotelian distinction, formal as well as material: not only did much of the content of his work ultimately derive from the heritage of the Reformation; but the principles of worship, as these had been worked out by Luther and his generation, provided much of the context for that work as well. Context, therefore, requires at least brief consideration alongside content. The distinctiveness of the Lutheran Reformation in its conception of the nature of worship, and therefore in its view of the place of music in the life of the church, had evolved out of its dual confrontation with Roman Catholicism and with Reformed Protestantism; and it was that dual confrontation, as complicated by the movements of eighteenth-century thought with which the next three chapters will be dealing, that continued to define what can perhaps be called its "philosophy of music" two centuries later, in Bach's time.[26]

According to Luther, worship was not exclusively a matter of forms. He regarded ceremonies as matters of indifference theologically, but he was not indifferent to ceremonies. Therefore he not only composed the hymns that we have been examining in his versions and Bach's revisions but he also published two orders of worship for the revised, "evangelical" form of the Mass: the Latin *Formula missae et communionis* in 1523, and the German *Deutsche Messe und Ordnung des Gottesdiensts* of 1526.[27] We shall be analyzing these two orders in more detail in chapter 9 because of their bearing on the composite work of Bach now called the *Mass in B Minor,* but for our purposes here they stand as part of the musical heritage of the Reformation because of the limitations that Luther's liturgical work placed on the church musician as both composer and performer as well as because of the opportunities that it provided for the church musician.

Probably no one has ever stated the limitations more directly and accurately than Paul Hindemith, who had reason to know at first hand the problems of the composer. In his lecture for the bicentenary of Bach's death in 1950, Hindemith pointed out that the church of the Lutheran Reformation "suffers from obvious weaknesses if one compares its musical possibilities to those of the Roman Catholic Church." For the musical heritage of the medieval church, based on the dominance of Gregorian chant, had required "practiced and practicing groups of singers . . . , striving for perfection in the true style of this music, a performance far removed from subjective expression and concert effectiveness." The result, paradoxically, could become the introduction into Protestant worship of "concert-like performances by professional musicians," which made "individual accomplishment the artistic determinant in the Protestant church."[28] One does not have to share Hindemith's harsh judgment on English Protestant hymnody to recognize that he has identified a genuine problem.

But that problem was, in many ways, the obverse side of the enormous effect that the Reformation had upon church music—and thus, to use Gérold's phrase, "upon the whole civilized world"—through its revival of congregational singing. The German chorale as we know it is a product of the later Middle Ages, with both Catholic and Hussite hymns making a substantial contribution. But it was with Luther and his Reformation that the chorale became a major historical force, also because Luther was far less reluctant than were his fellow Reformers to accept the hymnological and liturgical traditions of the preceding centuries. The very poverty that Hindemith describes made it obligatory to provide new music; the very teachings on which Luther and the Reformers insisted made it necessary to go beyond the adaptation and translation of existing hymns to the composition of new ones, already in the sixteenth but especially in the seventeenth century; the very theatricality whose dangers Hindemith so eloquently points out forced the domestication of concert-like performance by bringing it into the church and into the church service, as that domestication was carried out by Heinrich Schütz, Dietrich Buxtehude—and Johann Sebastian Bach.

Both the musical limitations and the musical opportunities coming out of Luther's Reformation represent the heritage that Bach received, but what he did to exploit the opportunities and to overcome the limitations represents his heritage to later generations. In Hindemith's moving words,

Recognition of human excellence in its highest form, knowledge of the path that leads to it, the necessary done with dutifulness and driven to that point of perfection where it outgrows all necessity—this knowledge is the most precious inheritance given us with Bach's music.[29]

3

Rationalism and *Aufklärung* in Bach's Career

Johann Sebastian Bach was a near contemporary of Voltaire, who, to many in his own time and in ours, "seems to embody the spirit of the Enlightenment in its assault upon the Church."[1] Voltaire was born, as François-Marie Arouet, in 1694, nine years after Bach, and died in 1778, twenty-eight years after Bach. What is more, not only did their lives intersect in time, their careers almost intersected in space as well. For from 1750, the year of Bach's death, to 1753, Voltaire resided at the court of Frederick the Great of Prussia. More than any other monarch, Frederick embodied the spirit of the German Enlightenment, or *Aufklärung*. He also, it has been said, "loved his country but despised its civilization . . . a Prussian who could never quite repress the wish that he had been born a Frenchman."[2] The one exception to Frederick's xenophilia was music, for, as the same scholar has commented, "music, in which the king took an abiding interest, was enjoying a minor domestic renaissance. . . . But music was unique."[3]

As the new Medici of this musical renaissance, Frederick the Great was himself a composer of not inconsiderable ability and a flutist of some prowess. He also emulated the *padroni* of the Cinquecento in drawing around himself as many talented people, like Voltaire, as he could. One of these, in May 1747, was J. S. Bach, in what Christoph Wolff has appropriately termed "one of the most notable biographical events in Bach's unspectacular life."[4] For as we shall have occasion to see again in chapter 6, Bach differed, in this respect as in many others, from his exact contemporary, George

.c Handel, who was an international celebrity. As Hans T. David and Arthur Mendel have noted, "His whole life was spent within one small area of Germany, bounded on the north by Lübeck and Hamburg, on the west by Cassel, on the south by Carlsbad, and on the east by Dresden."[5] We are fortunate to have, for Bach's appearance before the incumbent of the Prussian throne, a contemporary account from a Berlin newspaper, under date of 11 May 1747, which, despite its length, bears reciting in full:

> We hear from Potsdam that last Sunday [May 7] the famous Capellmeister from Leipzig, Mr. Bach, arrived with the intention of hearing the excellent Royal music at that place. In the evening, at about the time when the regular chamber music in the Royal apartments usually begins, His Majesty was informed that Capellmeister Bach had arrived at Potsdam and was waiting to listen to the music. His August Self immediately gave orders that Bach be admitted, and went, at his entrance, to the so-called "forte and piano," condescending also to play, in person and without any preparation, a theme to be executed by Capellmeister Bach in a fugue. This was done so happily by the aforementioned Capellmeister that not only His Majesty was pleased to show his satisfaction thereat, but also all those present were seized with astonishment. Mr. Bach has found the subject propounded to him so exceedingly beautiful that he intends to set it down on paper in a regular fugue and have it engraved on copper. On Monday, the famous man was heard on the organ in the Church of the Holy Ghost at Potsdam and earned general acclaim from the auditors attending in great number. In the evening, His Majesty charged him again with the execution of a fugue, in six parts, which he accomplished just as skillfully as on the previous occasion, to the pleasure of His Majesty and to the general admiration.[6]

Scholars have concluded that "the real original form of the 'thema regium,' as it was formulated by Frederick II on that memorable evening in the City Palace of Potsdam, is finally not verifiable."[7] But in a self-deprecatory letter to the king two months later, Bach professed to regret "that, for lack of necessary preparation, the execution of the task did not fare as well as such an excellent theme demanded"; and he dedicated to Frederick his *Musical Offering* [*Musikalisches Opfer*] (BWV 1079), which continues to attract the attention of Bach scholars because research on it has been "burdened with so many hypotheses."[8] This work "shows Bach elaborating on the theme supplied to him by Frederick the Great in every imaginable way for an ensemble of up to three instruments."[9]

As that anecdote suggests, Bach shared with the *Aufklärung* king of Prussia an enthusiasm for dazzling performance and a flair for the dramatic. In an anticipation of Romanticism's reverence for the genius, of which Goethe was to become the supreme idol and Thomas Carlyle's *Heroes and Hero-Worship* of 1841 and Ralph Waldo Emerson's *Representative Men* of 1850 the supreme expressions, the Enlightenment monarch, despite his rationalism, had a sense of awe and admiration in the presence of the keyboard virtuoso from Leipzig, despite his piety. That sense of awe and admiration transcends the borders of ideology and church, as Johannes Rüber makes clear in his novel *Bach and the Heavenly Choir*. This is, briefly, the story of a twentieth-century French abbot, an amateur violinist, who was elected pope and took the name of Gregory. Out of a variety of motives, ecumenical as well as artistic, Pope Gregory got the idea of canonizing Johann Sebastian Bach. After all the other obstacles to the canonization had been cleared away, there remained the challenge: "Had Johann Sebastian Bach fulfilled this apostolic commission" of performing miracles? In response,

> [Cardinal] Hopkins returned, carrying Gregory's violin case in its light canvas cover. . . . Gregory grasped his instrument and began to play the partita of Johann Sebastian. Again sound and light began their dance; the clear notes became as visible as light; movement, dance, became audible in the calm progress of the notes. Spellbound, they all watched that figure caught in the rhythm of the music, swaying to the natural time. . . . The Holy Father had made himself his own spokesman for his own candidate. . . . And it was as though, at that moment, theology had been defeated and the belief of the people had won the case on its own.[10]

So it was (uncomfortable though each of them might have been with the association) both with Pope Gregory and with King Frederick the Great: the virtuoso was a saint, regardless of theology (or, for that matter, anti-theology).

There are other affinities between this odd couple of Bach and Frederick the Great. One of them is an attitude of mind that Harry A. Wolfson, speaking about the differences between Spinoza and Descartes, has called the use of "mathematical analogies . . . as illustrations of the existence of inexorable laws of necessity throughout nature."[11] Since classical antiquity there had been a widespread belief that the laws of mathematics, of geometry but also of arithmetic, were a key to the meaning of the universe and even to the mystery of God. The Christian doctrine of the Trinity had provided the speculation of Augustine with a divinely revealed confirmation of the philosophical theory that "numbers . . . exist apart, a kind of galaxy in the mind's firmament."[12] The attitude of the *Aufklärung* toward this theory was ambivalent, as, in Ernst Cassirer's words, Enlightenment "philosophical thinking tries at the same time to separate itself from, and to hold fast to, mathematics; it seeks to free itself from the authority of mathematics, and yet in so doing not to contest or violate this authority but rather to justify it from a new angle."[13]

Music had long held a special place in the philosophical consideration of numerology. Augustine's *De musica,* and after it the mathematically oriented *De institutione musica* of Boethius, would dominate musical education, and much of musical theory, throughout the Middle Ages and into modern times. Thus we find Thomas Aquinas, in the very first question of his *Summa Theologica,* stating it as an axiom that "the science of perspective proceeds from principles established by geometry, and music from principles established by arithmetic," so that "the musician accepts on authority the principles taught him by the mathematician."[14] At the same time, the Middle Ages had also learned from Augustine about "the delights of the ear . . . in those melodies which thy words inspire when sung with a sweet and trained voice."[15] Bach's older contemporary, the English poet John Dryden, articulated both the mathematical and the emotional significance of music in the two odes he wrote on music for Saint Cecilia's Day. In 1687, two years after Bach's birth, Dryden affirmed the mathematical-musical structure of the cosmos:

> From harmony, from heavenly harmony,
> This universal frame began:
> When nature underneath a heap
> Of jarring atoms lay.[16]

But in his second ode for the patron saint of music, the familiar "Alexander's Feast: or The Power of Music" written when Bach was twelve years old, Dryden described how even before the invention of the organ, the musician, with

. . . his breathing flute
And sounding lyre,
Could swell the soul to rage or kindle soft desire.[17]

Thanks in part to the Romantic auspices under which the revival of Bach's cantatas and *Passions* was set in motion, we are accustomed to recognizing in his church music this latter quality of being able to "swell the soul."

Recently, however, scholars have begun to discuss as well the mathematical and numerological quality, not only in such avowedly virtuoso pieces as the *Musical Offering* for Frederick the Great but also in other works. It had been evident since studies early in this century that the forty-eight units of *The Well-Tempered Clavier* were based on an elaborately worked out and fundamentally mathematical conception of "symmetry of number and theme," on the basis of which the editor of Bach could correct existing copies.[18] And the "cyclical" nature of Bach's *Goldberg Variations* (*BWV* 988), obvious at one level even to the untrained ear of the amateur listener, has been shown to be both highly complex and integral to the very structure of the work. But Bach's sacred music, too, is suffused with numerological structures. This is discernible not merely in such obvious forms as the tenfold repetition of the leitmotiv in his setting (*BWV* 635) of Luther's hymn on the Ten Commandments, "Dies sind die heil'gen zehn Gebot [That man a godly life might live]" (*TLH* 287), but elsewhere. Thus Martin Jansen has examined the "number symbolism [*Zahlensymbolik*]" in Bach's *Passions,* suggesting how the repetition of certain intervals at crucial points in the narrative may be a representation of various of the traditional "sacred numbers" coming out of both the orthodox Christian and the less orthodox hermetic traditions; for example, the forty-three tones of Bach's setting in the *Matthew Passion* of the words of Christ (Matt. 26:29), "bis an den Tag [until that day]," correspond to the forty-three days between Maundy Thursday and Ascension Day.[19] One scholar has even tried to find in Bach's music a numerological dramatization of the orthodox Lutheran doctrine of "the communication of properties [*idiomatum communicatio*]" between the two natures in the person of Christ.[20] But in the consideration of possible influences of numerology and other theories on his compositions, it is salutary to remind ourselves of the statement in Bach's obituary: "Our lately departed Bach did not, it is true, occupy himself with deep theoretical speculations on music, but was all the stronger in the practice of the art."[21]

That disinclination to engage in "deep theoretical speculations," combined with a deep commitment to "the practice of the art," also formed an important aspect of Bach's relation to the *Aufklärung*. Therefore, as David and Mendel have noted, "As far as we know, he never wrote a word concerning the esthetic speculations or controversies of the time."[22] But they add that he did defend music against "a rector's attacks"; in fact, he did so more than once. The most revealing—and most amusing—of the several attacks to which Bach responded in his career was that of Johann August Ernesti, who assumed the post of rector (or headmaster) at the Thomasschule in 1734; he must be distinguished from a previous, and as far as we know unrelated, rector named Johann *Heinrich* Ernesti, to whom Bach referred as "the blessed late Rector Ernesti."[23] For just as in the period of the Enlightenment "for every deist Handel there was a devout Bach,"[24] so for every musician *manqué* like Frederick the Great (or, as he would undoubtedly have preferred, Frédéric le Grand) there was a Philistine like Johann August Ernesti. And while the fascination of such a figure as Voltaire or Thomas Jefferson has led historians of Enlightenment thought to stress its intellectual and theoretical accomplishments, it is important to balance the picture by keeping in view the pragmatism and utilitarianism in such fields as aesthetics and education that often accompanied Enlightenment skepticism about metaphysics and dogma.

Although it is certainly correct to say, as Peter Gay does, that "the philosophes' view of Enlightenment . . . was in essence pedagogic,"[25] they directed much of the pedagogy to the elimination not only of traditional learning but of useless knowledge (the two being often equated). Thus Benjamin Franklin founded "the American Philosophical Society" in 1744 but in 1766 replaced it with "the American Society for Promoting and Propagating *Useful Knowledge, Held in Philadelphia*"; the phrase "useful knowledge" survives in the eventual official name of the American Philosophical Society (APS), whose presidents included Benjamin Franklin himself as well as Thomas Jefferson. As the leading historian of the American Enlightenment has noted, one of the elements "in the common

APS ideology was a utilitarian conception of science," which expressed itself in the assumption "that any discovery of the workings of nature, even any particular fact, from a new plant to mastodon bones or Indian customs, was bound to prove useful to man."[26]

More than any other areas of human activity, it was the church and the arts that would feel the effect of such utilitarian pedagogy; therefore Johann Sebastian Bach, who represented both, was unavoidably on a collision course with this particular understanding of *Aufklärung*.[27] A recent study of the theological curriculum and clerical morale in eighteenth-century Germany has assembled a vast amount of documentary and anecdotal evidence about what it aptly terms "clerical utilitarianism" and the pressure that this utilitarian Rationalism put upon the church and the clergy to justify themselves before the forum of usefulness and practicality.[28] Preaching, the administration of the sacraments, and pastoral care were not sufficient to legitimate the ministry. Ministers were pressed into service as *Volkslehrer* and even teachers in elementary school, with emphasis on practical crafts like cobbling and blacksmithing, childrearing and home economics. The pulpit itself had to meet these criteria, and we have sermons for Palm Sunday that deal with the danger of tearing branches from trees just when the sap has begun to rise. Whatever did not point a practical moral lesson could be dismissed, for the way the pastor could make himself useful was "by helping the farmer to follow a better plan of life, by replacing superstitious quack medicines with truly effective remedies, and by giving prompt aid to those suffering from external lesions or wounds."[29] He could provide paralegal advice as well as para-agricultural and paramedical assistance.

In such an atmosphere, music—above all, church music—must have a difficult time. It would not be fair to identify the extremes of this utilitarianism with the viewpoint espoused by Johann August Ernesti, whose commitment to pure scholarship made him in some ways its opponent as well. It is evident from his subsequent career that his fundamental interests were scholarly and humanistic: in 1742 he received an appointment in "humane letters" at the University of Leipzig, and in 1756 he was elected to the professorship of rhetoric, to which then in 1759 a joint appointment to the faculty of theology was added.[30] When the sixteen-year-old

Goethe, who was born a year before Bach died, came to the University of Leipzig as a student in 1765, as he tells us in his autobiography, *Dichtung und Wahrheit*, "Ernesti appeared to me as a brilliant light." But he later comments that while he "learned something, indeed, from" Ernesti's lecture on Cicero, he "was not enlightened on the subject which particularly concerned me"; for he was in search of "a standard of opinion, and thought I perceived that nobody possessed it."[31] Ernesti was a Rationalist, almost against his will; and as, in his later career as a theological professor, he espoused a theological method according to which the grammatical meaning of the biblical text must take absolute precedence, so also, in his early career as "rector" or headmaster of a secondary school, he gave the study of philology and the humanities an exclusive position, at the cost of those areas which, had he been an educational reformer in twentieth-century America, he would certainly have described as "frills."

That was the intellectual and ideological source of the conflict between Bach and Ernesti.[32] But even a cursory review of "the flood of documents in this long drawn-out case,"[33] with their charges and countercharges, makes it clear that other than intellectual and ideological issues were involved. Not even Bach's most hagiographic admirers would dare to claim that this was his finest hour. He himself called the question a "trivial disciplinary and school matter," and Ernesti admitted that it was "not so great a thing."[34] A quarrel over the relative authority of rector and cantor in the hiring and firing of student prefects precipitated violent overreactions on both sides. Bach wrote out a bill of particulars against Ernesti on 12 August 1736, a second one on 13 August, a third one on 15 August, and a fourth one on 19 August; eventually he appealed to the consistory, and finally he appealed to the king of Saxony—about the assignment of a teaching assistant. Ernesti accused Bach of seeking "revenge," of attempting to justify himself by means of a "lie," and even of being willing to accept a bribe, claiming to have evidence that a gold coin "has made a soprano out of a boy that was no more a soprano than I am."

Ernesti did not, of course, claim to be a singer, but he did have decided opinions, if not clear qualifications, as a judge of musical ability and of its relative importance. And that, behind the conflict of personalities and the jockeying for "authority," "respect," and "obedience," was the substantive issue. Philipp Spitta speaks of Ernesti's "dull and pretentious aversion to music," and Albert Schweitzer (despite his own debts, as a New Testament scholar, to Ernesti's achievements in that field) calls him quite directly "an enemy of music."[35] It is not so much, apparently, that Ernesti was ignorant of music as that he placed it far below the level of the core curriculum of the Thomasschule; at the time, music occupied one-fifth of the course time and theology another one-fifth, on the principle that it was the purpose of the curriculum to combine music and theology in promoting piety and building character. As an almost contemporary account, written in 1776, tells us, "Bach began to hate those students who devoted themselves completely to the *humaniora* and treated music as a secondary matter"; on the other hand, Ernesti for his part "became a foe of music. When he came upon a student practicing on an instrument, he would exclaim: 'What? You want to be a beer-fiddler, too?'"[36] He accused Bach of a musical snobbery that made him think it was "beneath his dignity to conduct at a wedding service where only chorales were to be sung" instead of entire cantatas. Moreover, he did not credit Bach's judgment of musical talent very highly. Referring to the sacking of the student prefect, he maintained that "Mr. Bach cannot instance anything but his incompetence, because he thinks not only that he will be conceded the right to pass such a judgment, but that it will be held in this case to be correct and unbiased." With utter insouciance, Ernesti expressed the opinion that the student prefect in question had an "excellent talent," and even took an oath that Bach had admitted, "Oh, I suppose he's competent enough!"

Bach had indeed instanced "merely" the young man's incompetence, complaining that, in addition to being (as Ernesti agreed) "a dissolute dog" and a spendthrift, the prefect had an unreliable sense of meter and "could not accurately give the beat in the two principal kinds of time." Bach was, in short, "fully convinced of his incompetence," especially when it came to giving the beat for "the concerted pieces that are performed by the First Choir, which are mostly of my own composition [and] are incomparably harder and more intricate than those that are sung by the Second Choir (and this only on Feast Days)." As cantor of the Thomasschule and composer of the cantatas being presented by its First Choir, he believed that he had both the authority and the responsibility to be "chiefly guided, in the choice of [the members of the choir], by the *capacité* of those who are to perform [his own compositions]." This was, in short, a confrontation between "music" and "learning," to use Spitta's terms, part of a process whose eventual outcome in the nineteenth century was that "at last our very greatest poets and most learned men regarded music with indifference or contempt."[37] Thus Frederick the Great and Ernesti represent the two opposite poles of *Aufklärung* thought in relation to music, and Bach's encounter with Ernesti and his encounter with Frederick the Great represent the two major points in his career when he was forced to clarify his stance toward Enlightenment Rationalism.

A full appreciation of that stance, however, must come not only from the biographical notices about Bach's career that we have been citing but also from his music itself. For as it is in such so-called secular compositions as the *Musical Offering* dedicated to Frederick the Great or *The Art of the Fugue* that Bach's affinities with Enlightenment Rationalism are most discernible, so it must also be in his church music, perhaps even more than in the data of his biography, that his differences from the *Aufklärung* become visible (or audible). While many of the specific differences will be concerning us in subsequent chapters as we deal with specific themes (for example, in chapter 7, the difference between Bach's reading of the Gospel story in *The Passion according to Saint Matthew* and the beginnings, at the very same time, of what Schweitzer calls "the quest of the historical Jesus"), we must look here, if only briefly, at the most fundamental difference of all.

One of the most recent historical assessments of the thought of Johann August Ernesti and its influence, that of Emanuel Hirsch, has concluded:

> It is more as a philologist and a historian than as a theologian that Ernesti interprets Scripture. The content of the New Testament does not represent to him a mystery that discloses itself only to a specific spiritual experience, but a reality that is simply taken to be "there" in a positivistic sense, for whose understanding nothing more is demanded than impartial human sense and a reverence in the face of that which is given as a matter of fact.[38]

This judgment of Ernesti does not mean to say that he was consciously altering the traditional biblical picture from a three-dimensional to a two-dimensional one by eliminating the dimension of mystery, or that he was aware of reducing the mystery of faith to a positivistic system of reality. Ernesti objected, frequently and consistently, that this was not what he was doing. Yet that was the wave of the theological future in the second half of the eighteenth century: Ernesti represented that future, in spite of himself, and he rode that wave.

But in this respect, Bach represented the past. In the presence of the biblical message, his response is not the "reverence in the face of that which is given as a matter of fact" of which Hirsch speaks in describing Ernesti's method of interpretation, but a reverence that makes the text its own. For Bach

> believed that the biblical text was designed to release within the reader an intense kind of spiritual activity. The interpreter must therefore help the text produce in his own audience an emotional action appropriate to the text at hand. He should give priority not to the axis between the Gospel and other ancient books, nor between each successive sentence and the biblical author's conscious and literal intent, but to that [axis] between the events narrated and the contemporary audience whose members are called on to respond to those events in unqualified immediacy and with their whole being.[39]

This is, it must perhaps be added in anticipation of our final chapter, not the same as maintaining that Bach's own inner being, in its "immediacy," was unqualifiedly expressing itself in each of his texts.

One example, selected almost (but not quite) at random from hundreds, is the cantata (*BWV* 108) "Es ist euch gut, dasz ich hingehe [It is for you that I depart now]" (Ambrose, *Cantatas* 270–72), based on the words of Jesus in John 16:7 and composed for the Fourth Sunday after Easter, 29 April 1725. After the tenor has sung those words from the Gospel, the bass responds:

> Mich kann kein Zweifel stören,
> Auf dein Wort, Herr, zu hören.
> Ich glaube, gehst du fort,
> So kann ich mich getrösten,
> Dasz ich zu den Erlösten
> Komm an erwünschten Port.

[There shall no doubt deter me
To thy word, Lord, I'll hearken.
I trust that if thou go'st,
I can in this find comfort,
That I'll, amongst the rescued
Come, at the welcome port.]

This must not be taken to mean, as Bach's simple-minded champions and his detractors have both sometimes maintained, that, even in the face of the rationalistic critique of the biblical message by the *Aufklärung*, his was a placid and unruffled faith. Repeatedly in his works, both in the texts and in the music, we can hear echoes of the Credo that has, ever since the Rationalism of the *Aufklärung*, been the way moderns have confessed their faith, employing the words of the father of the demoniac child in the Gospel of Mark (9:24), who, we are told, "cried out [with tears] and said, 'I believe; help my unbelief!'" That very text is the theme of the following cantata (*BWV* 109), "Ich glaube, lieber Herr, hilf meinem Unglauben [I have faith, O dear Lord, help my unbelieving]" (Ambrose, *Cantatas 272-74*). And in the cantata (*BWV* 78) "Jesu, der du meine Seele [Jesus, thou who this my spirit]" (Ambrose, *Cantatas 200-203*)—whose opening chorus is a reminder of the "Crucifixus" in the *Mass in B Minor* and whose duet for treble voices, "Wir eilen [We hasten]," is often performed by itself or even transcribed for instruments alone[40]—the closing chorale prays:

Herr! Ich glaube, hilf mir Schwachen,
Lasz mich ja verzagen nicht;
Du, du kannst mich stärker machen,
Wenn mich Sünd' und Tod anficht.

[Lord, I trust thee, help my weakness,
Let me, yea, not know despair.
Thou, thou canst my strength make firmer
When by sin and death I'm vexed.]

But probably the most dramatic expression of Bach's relation to the *Aufklärung*, and one that has been the subject of so much homiletical embellishment and myth-making that fact and fiction are inseparable, is the organ chorale that is usually regarded as his final work, which is appended to *The Art of the Fugue* and now bears the number *BWV* 668 in the Schmieder catalogue: "Vor deinen Thron tret ich hiermit [And now I step before thy throne]." The melody was the familiar sixteenth-century hymn by Paul Eber, "Wenn wir in höchsten Nöthen sind [When in the hour of deepest need]" (*LBW* 303).[41] Bach had used the melody before—for example, in two chorales (*BWV* 431 and 432), and even as early as 1714 (*BWV* 641). Now, as he lay blind and dying in July 1750, he returned to it, dictating to his son-in-law, Johann Christoph Altnikol. Schweitzer's poignant telling of the story is well known,[42] but here is another hagiographic account, by the French scholar André Pirro:

> In July, 1750, his eyes seemed to acquire a new lease of life; he could gradually see. . . . But it was the approaching splendor of death which radiated in him. . . . He had been working almost to the last moment with his son-in-law Altnikol, dictating a chorale for organ on the hymn *Wenn wir in höchsten Nöthen sind* (When we are in direst need). But he changed the title and, instead of these words of distress, he wrote: *Vor deinem* [*sic*] *Thron tret' ich hiemit* [*sic*] (I will appear before thy Throne). This was his last prayer and the last offering of his devout spirit.[43]

In the familiar Italian proverb, "Se non è vero, è molto ben trovato [If it isn't true, it's a delightful fiction]"; or, It may not be accurate but it is still true. For after having stood before the most enlightened throne of the *Aufklärung* at Potsdam three years before and having demonstrated to the king there both his brilliant rationality and his virtuosity, he now stood before another Throne and another King, who dwelt indeed in rationality but even more in mystery. And in the words of one of Bach's young theological protégés, "All that the advocates of materialism could bring forward must collapse before this one example."[44]

4
Confessional Orthodoxy
in Bach's Religion

Among the contemporary theologians with whom Bach was personally acquainted—who, as we have seen in chapter 3, included, much to their mutual regret, the philologist and New Testament scholar Johann August Ernesti—the one who made the most direct contribution to Bach as a church musician was certainly Erdmann Neumeister. He was born in 1671, fourteen years before Bach, and died at the age of eighty-five in 1756, six years after Bach. Most of his ministry was spent in Hamburg, where he came in 1715 and remained for more than forty years. Neumeister is the author of over two hundred books, some of them running to many hundreds of pages each. Not only was he a poet of considerable ability, he was also a literary critic: his treatise *On German poets* [*De poetis germanicis*] is an important landmark in the early history of modern literary theory, as a recent scholarly edition of it has shown.[1]

Neumeister was the chief pastor of the Jacobi-Kirche in Hamburg when Bach applied for the position of organist there in November 1720. It seems clear that the principal reason why Bach failed to receive the appointment was the practice that obtained there of expecting the appointee to make a substantial financial contribution to the church. This was, they assured everyone, not to be construed as buying the position, which, as part of the ministry of the church, could be purchased only by running great danger of the sin of simony. But, according to the minutes of its meeting of 21 November 1720, the search committee that considered Bach and his rivals decided that "if, after the selection has been made, the chosen candidate of his own free will wished to give a token of his gratitude, the latter could be accepted."[2] Nonetheless, a contemporary narrative, by one Johann Mattheson in *Der musicalische Patriot*, leaves no doubt either about the true nature of the financial transaction or about Neumeister's indignant reaction, even though no names are mentioned. Although Bach had "aroused universal admiration for his artistry," one of his rivals "was better at preluding with his thalers than with his fingers" and got the job. Neumeister was shocked and angered, and he took the occasion of the upcoming Christmas holiday, on the basis of the Gospel story in the second chapter of Luke, to suggest from his pulpit that "even if one of the angels of Bethlehem should come down from Heaven, one who played divinely and wished to become organist of St. Jacobi, but had no money, he might just as well fly away again."[3]

Neumeister's place in Bach's career goes far beyond that anecdote, however. As an anonymous contemporary foreword to the collection of his poetical works put it, Neumeister was "without doubt the first creator of the cantata."[4] Another contemporary, Gottfried Tilgner, called him "the man who, without contradiction, deserves the fame of being the first among us Germans who brought church music to a higher standing by introducing the sacred cantata and bringing it to its present perfection."[5] Even his detractors are obliged to grant that "as a poet Neumeister occupies a notable place, and his gift of poetic intuition and of light and fluent language must be acknowledged."[6] What those detractors seem hard put to understand is how and why Neumeister could have combined with this poetic talent a theological position that was so unqualifiedly orthodox. The preface to his poems noted that "you will certainly find nothing here that is not orthodox and in conformity with sound evangelical doctrine," and near the end of his life Neumeister himself declared that in the fifty-four years of his ministry he had "throughout the time I held this office striven to love that orthodoxy which the present world in its wisdom hates, and to instruct all my hearers in it."[7] He lamented the neglect of orthodox doctrine in his time, as "the children of Belial made one breach after another" in the walls of confessional orthodoxy, and he prayed that the church "might be edified through the sound doctrine of the almighty and eternal word of God."[8] He had put his poems, hymns, and cantatas at the service of that orthodoxy, and he believed that thereby he stood in continuity with both the hymnody and the theological orthodoxy of confessional Lutheranism.

An epitome of both the hymnody and the confessional orthodoxy was Luther's hymn of 1542, "Erhalt' uns, Herr, bei deinem Wort."[9] Luther himself called it "a children's song, to be sung in opposition to the two archenemies of Christ and of his church, the Pope and the Turk":

> Erhalt' uns, Herr, bei deinem Wort
> Und steur' des Pabsts und Türken Mord,
> Die Jesum Christum, deinen Sohn,
> Wollten stürzen von seinem Thron.

An early English hymnal in America rendered those first two lines quite literally:

> Lord, keep us in Thy Word and work,
> Restrain the murd'rous Pope and Turk.

By 1941, however, hymnody, if not theology, was prepared to mollify Luther's polemic against "the two archenemies of Christ and of his church," and the revised version of that hymnal adopted Catherine Winkworth's translation of 1863, which is now in general use:

> Lord, keep us steadfast in Thy Word;
> Curb those who fain by craft and sword
> Would wrest the Kingdom from Thy Son
> And set at naught all He hath done. (*TLH* 261)

Neumeister had no such compunctions. He defended "Erhalt' uns, Herr" against the accusation that is was "a hymn of mockery, filled with calumny and blasphemy."[10] And Bach had no such compunctions either, for in 1725 he composed a cantata based on Luther's hymn (*BWV* 126), "Erhalt uns, Herr, bei deinem Wort [Maintain us, Lord, within thy word]" (Ambrose, *Cantatas* 308–10).[11] That cantata, interpreted on the one hand in the light of his other works and on the other hand in the light of the works of such orthodox Lutheran theologians as Erdmann Neumeister, can help to illumine the place of confessional orthodoxy in Bach's religion. For further documentation of Bach's orthodoxy we are fortunate to have in this country

Bach's own copy of the three-volume annotated German Bible of the most stalwart of all the defenders of Lutheran Orthodoxy, Abraham Calovius (1612–86), with marginalia in Bach's hand.[12] Following the precedent of many of Neumeister's sermons, it would seem only right to consider the topic of Bach's confessional orthodoxy under three subheads: the absoluteness of Christianity; the doctrine of justification as the formal principle of the Reformation; and the authority of Scripture in opposition to the "pride" of human reason as the material principle of the Reformation.

The absoluteness of Christianity had been the fundamental presupposition of all Christian orthodoxy from the beginning. The exclusionary principle stated in the New Testament formula, "There is salvation in no one else, for there is no other name under heaven given among men by which we must be saved,"[13] was under attack in Bach's time. His younger contemporary, Gotthold Ephraim Lessing (1729–81), would, in the parable of the three rings in his *Nathan der Weise* of 1779, rule the question of absoluteness out of court. On all sides in the first half of the eighteenth century, the champions of orthodoxy in all denominations felt themselves to be embattled by the principal intellectual movements of the time. A primary focus of the attack, and therefore of the defense, was the doctrine of the Trinity. Enlightenment critics were concerned to demonstrate that neither the Old Testament nor even the New Testament supported the orthodox version of that doctrine. Such supposed proofs as the plural "Let us make man in our image" in the creation story (Gen. 1:26) and the threefold Aaronitic benediction (Num. 6:24–26) were reading an orthodox Christian interpretation back into the Hebrew Bible. Similarly, the famous "Johannine comma" of 1 John 5:7, "There are three that bear record in heaven, the Father, the Word, and the Holy Ghost: and these three are one," was a later interpolation into the New Testament.

Bach's copy of Calov's annotated Bible, by contrast, insisted that the Second Commandment of the Mosaic Decalogue in Ex. 20:3 meant "that we must accept, acknowledge, and honor only the Holy Trinity as God, and put our trust in him."[14] And 1 John 5:7, "which has occasioned more conflict than any other passage in Holy Scripture," nevertheless served Neumeister as the basis for a sermon vigorously defending the doctrine of the Trinity, in which he asserted that he had "not the slightest doubt that Saint John really wrote it."[15] With its corollary doctrine of the divine nature of Christ, the doctrine of the Trinity became for Neumeister the key to interpreting the Old Testament and the New.[16] Bach's use of the doctrine of the Trinity seems to have assigned it a similar place, as two examples from among many in his works will suggest. The chorale preludes for organ (*BWV* 669-768) that constitute the third part of Bach's *Clavier-Übung* are entitled "various preludes on the hymns of the Catechism." The chorale prelude (*BWV* 552) for the "Saint Anne's Chorale," best known to us from its (later) words, "O God, our help in ages past," serves as the "frame [*Rahmen*]" for these Catechism Preludes. But the first six (*BWV* 669-74) are permutations of the medieval German hymn, "Kyrie, Gott Vater in Ewigkeit," which addresses the "Kyrie eleison" successively to each of the three persons of the Trinity. And the climax of the entire series is Bach's infinitely complex and yet perfectly simple prelude and fughetta based on Luther's German setting of the Nicene Creed, "Wir glauben all' an einen Gott' (*BWV* 680-81), discussed in an earlier chapter.[17] It is difficult to see these preludes, and the trinitarian credo to which they give voice, as anything but the center not only of part 3 of the *Clavier-Übung* but of Bach's confession.

Although we shall be turning to the detailed consideration of Bach's *Mass in B Minor* in chapter 9, it would be impossible to discuss his trinitarian orthodoxy here without at least brief attention to its setting of the Nicene Creed. Leaving aside for the present such aspects of the Creed as the reciprocal musical relation between the "Et resurrexit" that declares the resurrection of Christ and the "Et expecto resurrectionem mortuorum" that affirms the Christian hope of the universal resurrection, we may turn for a moment to the duet for soprano and alto, "Et in unum Dominum." For as the two voices weave back and forth, they echo and reecho the phrases of the Creed, "*Deum de Deo, lumen de lumine, Deum verum de Deo vero*, [God *of* God, light *of* light, true God *of* true God]." Even Albert Schweitzer, with his intense hostility to the orthodox doctrines of the Trinity and the person of Christ, finds the theology impressive:

The theologian Bach also had a hand in the composition of the *Credo*. He knew what the Greek fathers had in their minds when they took

46

such pains to prove the identity of Christ with God and yet assert a diversity and independence of persons. To the dogmatist Bach the parallel passages . . . were not merely empty sounds to be turned into music; he knew what the formulae meant, and translated them into terms of music. He makes both singers sing the same notes, but in such a way that it does not amount to the same thing; the voices follow each other in strict canonic imitation; the one proceeds out of the other just as Christ proceeds out of God. . . . Bach thus proves that the dogma can be expressed much more clearly and satisfactorily in music than in verbal formulae.[18]

As in his setting of Luther's hymn on the Creed, so also here Bach made his own the trinitarian orthodoxy of the church fathers and of the Reformers.

An integral component of trinitarian orthodoxy was the legitimacy of addressing prayer and worship not only to God the Father but to the Trinity, and therefore also to the Son and the Holy Spirit. We had occasion earlier to comment briefly on the hymns and prayers to the Holy Spirit, most of them adaptations of the "Veni, Creator Spiritus" and "Veni, Sancte Spiritus" of the Middle Ages, on which Luther had based several hymns and on which, in turn, Bach had based chorale preludes.[19] In the present context, it is the appropriateness of praying to Jesus Christ as the Second Person of the Trinity that pervades much of Bach's sacred music. Wolfgang Schmieder's orderly mind, which arranged several of the groups of Bach chorales more or less alphabetically, has made it convenient to run some rough statistical analyses. Thirty-one of the 189 chorales to which he assigned *BWV* 250–438, or almost exactly one-sixth, are addressed in their opening line to Jesus; that does not include those that shift to some such locution later. Of the seventy chorales (*BWV* 599–668) in the *Orgel-Büchlein*, twenty, or almost one-third, are prayers to Jesus.

Bach's cantatas and motets too are a vindication of this orthodox doctrine and practice. "Jesu, meine Freude" (*BWV* 227) is an elaborate and stirring celebration of the orthodox confidence in Jesus Christ. One of Bach's early cantatas (*BWV* 61), composed in 1714 at Weimar and based on Luther's "Nun komm, der Heiden Heiland [Now come, the gentiles' Savior]" (Ambrose, *Cantatas* 157–59), which was based in turn on the "Veni, Redemptor gentium" of Ambrose, was a work of Erdmann Neumeister; it put into verse and aria the interpretations of Advent quoted from Neumeister in chapter 1 above, and did so in the form of a prayer to Christ, as "the gentiles' Savior," to come in grace as he once came in the flesh and as he would come in glory. The same petition dominates the exquisitely lyrical dialogue between Christ and the soul in the cantata (*BWV* 140) "Wachet auf [Wake, arise]" (Ambrose, *Cantatas* 339–41):[20]

> Seele: Wenn kommst du, mein Heil?
> Jesus: Ich komme, dein Teil.
> Seele: Ich warte mit brennendem Öle.
> Eröffne den Saal
> Zum himmlischen Mahl!
> Jesus: Ich öffne den Saal
> Zum himmlischen Mahl.
> Seele: Komm, Jesu!
> Jesus: Ich komme; komm, liebliche Seele!
>
> [Soul: When com'st thou, my Savior?
> Jesus: I'm coming, thy share.
> Soul: I'm waiting with my burning oil.
> Now open the hall
> For heaven's rich meal.
> Jesus: I open the hall.
> For heaven's rich meal.
> Soul: Come, Jesus!
> Jesus: Come, O lovely soul!]

And then there follows, with one of Bach's most famous accompaniments, the second stanza of Philipp Nicolai's hymn, the tenor chorale, "Zion hört die Wächter singen [Zion hears the watchmen singing]," whose climax is the cry:

> Nun komm, du werte Kron,
> Herr Jesu, Gottes Sohn,
> Hosianna!
>
> [Now come, thou precious crown,
> Lord Jesus, God's own Son!
> Hosanna pray!]

The orthodox doctrine of the Trinity had originally evolved as a way of providing justification for the incurable practice that Christians had, apparently from the very beginning, of worshiping Jesus as divine.[21] Now the process had come full circle: the evolved doctrine of trinitarian orthodoxy was inspiring further expressions of that ancient practice. And the trinitarian declaration of the absoluteness of the revelation in Christ was expressing itself in such a prayer to Christ as the second stanza of Luther's "Erhalt' uns, Herr":

> Beweis' dein Macht, Herr Jesu Christ,
> Der du Herr aller Herren bist:
> Beschirm' dein' arme Christenheit,
> Dasz sie dich lob' in Ewigkeit.

> [Lord Jesus Christ, Thy power make known,
> For Thou art Lord of lords alone:
> Defend Thy Christendom that we
> May evermore sing praise to Thee.] (*TLH* 261.2)

That was a prayer *to* Christ, but it was also a prayer *against* "the murd'rous Pope and Turk." Orthodoxy, therefore, had taken on an additional and a more specific meaning in Bach's tradition. It was "confessional" orthodoxy because its principal authority, besides the Holy Scriptures that all Christians shared, was the *Book of Concord* of 1580, the collection of the confessional books of the Lutheran Church. Thus when Bach was called as organist to Halle in 1713, he was charged in the very first paragraph of the call that he should "above all cling faithfully all his life long to the unchanged Augsburg Confession, the Formula of Concord, and other symbolic confessions of faith."[22] Bach seems, "all his life long," to have been comfortable with this requirement of confessional subscription and, as we have seen earlier, made a major contribution to the observance of the bicentenary of the Augsburg Confession by composing cantatas for three successive days in 1730; on the other hand, as we shall have occasion to note several times later, he was also comfortable with his basically "secular" duties at Cöthen, where the Calvinist rather than the Lutheran version of Protestantism enjoyed official favor. Two of the Lutheran confessions contained in the *Book of Concord* were the Small and the Large Catechisms, written by Luther himself. We referred earlier to the chorale preludes composed by Bach at Leipzig in 1739 as part 3 of his *Clavier-Übung,* which he called "various preludes on the hymns of the Catechism," namely, of course, Luther's Catechism as contained in the *Book of Concord.* For Bach and for his church, therefore, the Catechism was a manual (*Enchiridion,* as Luther called it) for the instruction of young and old; it was a confession of the specifically Lutheran doctrine; and it was, through the hymns based upon it, an expression of the church's worship—all three of these at the same time.

In addition to the Catechisms, only one other of the Lutheran Confessions had been written by Luther himself, the Smalcald Articles of 1537. In the Smalcald Articles, Luther had declared, and the Lutheran Church with him, "that the pope is the real Antichrist who has raised himself over and set himself against Christ."[23] The Rationalism of Bach's time was profoundly ambivalent about such polemics. For on the one hand it was a common practice among *Aufklärung* thinkers to use Roman Catholicism as a whipping boy for attacks upon all institutional churches and all supernatural religion. "Priestcraft [*Klerisey* in German]" was blamed for holding the people in superstition and ignorance, and it was therefore the hope of some in the anticlerical Enlightenment to see "the last king strangled with the guts of the last priest."[24] In places like Bach's Saxony, the real object of such attacks upon clericalism was, of course, the Protestant-Lutheran establishment, even though the explicit language referred to Roman Catholicism. On the other hand, the impulse to religious toleration, for which the Enlightenment marched in the vanguard, professed to find all polemical language, even that against Roman Catholicism, offensive—although it should perhaps be added that even in such progressive centers of Enlightenment thought and religious toleration as England and America, Roman Catholicism and Judaism were the last to be accorded recognition. The *Aufklärung* hoped to root out the religious hatred and dogmatic controversy that had reached their peak in the Reformation and its aftermath. Therefore, for example, the orthodox Erdmann Neumeister was obliged to defend himself against the charge "that I have preached and written too severely [*allzuscharff*] against other religions and have not manifested any love to them."[25]

The many chorale preludes and cantatas that Bach composed for the celebration of the Feast of the Reformation certainly are an indication that this polemical accent of Lutheran confessional orthodoxy was not alien to him. "Polemical" comes from the Greek word *polemos*, "war," and the metaphors of war seem to have come easily to Bach specifically when he set out to vindicate the Reformation. One of the most warlike of his arias, therefore, occurs specifically within the context of the cantata he composed on Luther's "battle hymn of the Reformation" (*BWV* 80), "Ein' feste Burg ist unser Gott [A mighty fortress is our God]" (Ambrose, *Cantatas* 205–8). After the chorus has sung the third stanza of that chorale, the tenor recitative issues the following summons:

> So stehe dann bei Christi blutgefärbten Fahne,
> O Seele, fest
> Und glaube, dasz dein Haupt dich nicht verläszt,
> Ja dasz dein Sieg
> Auch dir den Weg zu deiner Krone bahne!
> Tritt freudig an den Krieg!
> Wirst du nur Gottes Wort
> So hören als bewahren,
> So wird der Feind gezwungen auszufahren,
> Dein Heiland bleibt dein Hort!

> [So stand under Christ's bloodstained flag and banner,
> O spirit, firm,
> And trust that this thy head betrays thee not,
> His victory
> E'en thee the way to gain thy crown prepareth!
> March gladly on to war!
> If thou but God's own word
> Obey as well as hearken,
> Then shall the foe be forced to leave the battle;
> Thy Saviour is thy shield.]

All the language about the devil, both in Luther's chorale and in Bach's cantata, could mean that the *Feind* against whom this recitative is directed is Satan; but the emphasis on hearing the word of God and keeping it, and indeed the very setting of the cantata, makes it at least worthy of consideration that Luther's "Ein' feste Burg," like Luther's "Erhalt' uns, Herr," was being sung "against the archenemies of Christ and of his church," and particularly against the Pope and Roman Catholicism.

Bach's loyalty to Reformation anti-Catholicism as an expression of confessional orthodoxy also expressed itself in the many and varied affirmations, throughout his works, of what a later generation would call the "formal principle" and the "material principle" of the Reformation, the doctrine of justification by faith alone and the doctrine of the sole authority of Scripture, or, to use the standard

Latin slogans, *sola fide* and *sola Scriptura*. These same two Reformation principles, moreover, represented the bulwarks of confessional orthodoxy also against Enlightenment Rationalism.

The Reformation doctrine of justification by faith alone, without works, had been, in Luther's eyes, his fundamental discovery, as he pondered the message of the Bible, and above all the epistles of Paul. So completely did Luther make his own the Pauline argumentation on justification that the two are often identified. As Neumeister put it in one of his anti-Catholic polemical sermons, "the papists are completely hostile to [Paul], and if they had their way they would throw his epistles out of the Bible, particularly those to the Romans and the Galatians."[26] Luther had given expression to the doctrine of justification in various of his hymns, although none of them had dealt primarily with that doctrine. Thus in the hymn that forms the basis for Bach's chorale preludes *BWV* 311 and 312, "Es woll' uns Gott genädig sein," Luther had prayed for the unearned gift of grace, which was the foundation of justification.

But the most detailed treatment of justification in Reformation hymnody, a chorale that forms the basis for a Bach cantata (*BWV* 9) composed for the Sixth Sunday after Trinity sometime in the 1730s, was not written by Luther himself, although it was included in the hymnal *Etlich christlich Lieder* published at Wittenberg in 1524: "Es ist das Heil uns kommen her [Now is to us salvation come]" (Ambrose, *Cantatas* 40–42). The original hymn was written by Luther's colleague Paul Speratus, Lutheran bishop of Pomerania and Luther's collaborator in compiling the hymnal of 1524.[27] Unlike most of Luther's hymns, the twelve stanzas of this chorale are overtly doctrinal, one might say even technically theological, in language as well as in content, being cast as a paraphrase of the argumentation about law and justification in the first three chapters of the Epistle to the Romans:

> Salvation unto us has come
> By God's free grace and favor;
> Good works cannot avert our doom,
> They help and save us never.
> Faith looks to Jesus Christ alone,
> Who did for all the world atone;
> He is our mediator. (*LBW* 297)

What Bach does is to take that opening stanza and the doxology that forms the closing twelfth stanza, and make these two the "frame" for his cantata. Speratus's stanzas surround an elaborately worked out set of madrigals and a canonic duet.[28]

The other Reformation principle, *sola Scriptura,* was also directed against human pride and pretension, insisting that only through the divine revelation contained in the Bible was it possible to learn the truth about God. Although Luther did not, consistently or simple-mindedly, identify the Bible with the word of God, the opening line of the chorale "Erhalt' uns, Herr, bei deinem Wort" would appear at least to include the Bible in its definition of the word. When Bach and his librettist, who seems to be unidentified, set about expanding the three stanzas of Luther's "children's song, to be sung in opposition to the two archenemies of Christ and of his church, the Pope and the Turk," into a full-scale cantata, it was this dual emphasis of the Reformation on the primacy of divine grace and the authority of divine revelation that they seized upon. Therefore Bach has an aria in this cantata, "Stürze zu Boden, schwülstige Stolze [Crash down in ruin, arrogant bombast!]" (Ambrose, *Cantatas* 309), which graphically describes the vain efforts of human reason and human morality to rise by their own effort. In this aria "he is not content merely to depict the fall, but shows us repeated efforts to rise again, until there comes the final plunge."[29] Earlier in the cantata, the rescuing power of grace and revelation is celebrated in a tenor aria, accompanied by two oboes, "Sende deine Macht von oben [Send down thy great strength from heaven]," which indeed "seems like a heavenly choir singing the praise of God."[30]

Neumeister evidently saw in the Reformation doctrine of the word a weapon against the twin dangers of Rationalism and Roman Catholicism. Into his devotional book of 1737 on Advent, he inserted a verse, obviously of his own composition, praising the Bible as inspired and inerrant:

> Es stimmt ja in allen Sachen
> Die liebe Bibel überein.
> So hab ich diesen Schlusz zu machen:
> Sie musz ein Buch von Himmel seyn;
> Darinnen man kein Wort nicht liest,
> Das nicht die Wahrheit Gottes ist.

[The Bible is, in everything,
Free of contradiction.
And so I must conclude
That it is a book from heaven,
In which there is not a single word
That is not the very truth of God.][31]

But Neumeister was not content to employ his poetic talents in support of the inspiration of Scripture only in such a private writing. On the basis of the words of Isa. 56:10–11, celebrating the fruitfulness of the word of God, which "shall not return to me empty," he worked out a cantata (*BWV* 18), "Gleichwie der Regen und Schnee vom Himmel fällt [Just as the showers and snow from heaven fall]" (Ambrose, *Cantatas* 60–62), which Bach set to music perhaps as early as 1713 but certainly by 1715.[32] Sometime later Neumeister wrote another cantata, based on the saying of Jesus in John 14:23, "Wer mich liebet, der wird mein Wort halten [He who loves me will keep my commandments]" (Ambrose, *Cantatas* 553–54). This was apparently the first cantata (*BWV* 59) that Bach performed publicly at Leipzig when he "took up his duties" there, perhaps on 16 May 1723.[33] Two years later, on Pentecost 1725, the cantata was reworked and presented again, forming now number 74 in the Schmieder listing (Ambrose, *Cantatas* 188–90). Originally, the emphasis on the word of God in Luther's "Erhalt' uns, Herr, bei deinem Wort" had been directed above all against the claim of Roman Catholicism that the church was, along with the Scriptures, a "source of revelation" and that therefore only the church's interpretation of the Scriptures was valid. But now it was necessary to refine that emphasis also against the claim of reason being set forth by the Enlightenment. Therefore the denunciation of the "schwülstige Stolze" in Bach's cantata.

In spite of all this close collaboration with Erdmann Neumeister and the obvious sympathy that Bach manifested for the central emphases of confessional orthodoxy, it would be a mistake—and one into which latter-day champions of confessional orthodoxy have all too easily fallen[34] —simply to equate his position with that of orthodox theologians like Neumeister. We shall have occasion in later chapters to return to two of the basic ways in which Bach's church music diverges from the strictness of late seventeenth-century Lutheran Orthodoxy. Bach's *Magnificat* and his *Mass in B Minor* both manifest an "evangelical catholicity" that would be difficult to square with an authoritarian and anti-Catholic confessional orthodoxy. And in the next chapter, when we discuss "pietism, piety, and devotion in Bach's cantatas," we shall see that the Pietism that was Neumeister's bête noire does in fact play a prominent role in the texts, and even in the music, of many of Bach's cantatas. Nevertheless, the central trinitarian affirmation of confessional orthodoxy—and, for that matter, of "evangelical catholicity," and perhaps even of Pietism—was fundamental to Bach's faith.

5

Pietism, Piety, and Devotion
in Bach's Cantatas

In July 1694, when Bach was nine years old, there took place what the most authoritative modern encyclopedia of Protestant theology does not hesitate to call "an event of epoch-making significance," the establishment of the University of Halle, which almost immediately became, under the leadership of August Hermann Francke (1663–1727), the major intellectual and theological center of the movement called Pietism.[1] Thus the early years of Johann Sebastian Bach were also the mature years of the two principal founders of Pietism, Francke and Philipp Jacob Spener (1635–1705). A member of Bach's own generation, though fifteen years younger than he, was Spener's godson, Nikolaus Ludwig Graf von Zinzendorf (1700–60), the Saxon nobleman who is best remembered for having founded the Moravian Church of Herrnhut, or Unitas Fratrum, to whose rich heritage of hymnody English-speaking Christianity, particularly through the Wesleyan tradition, owes such a great debt.[2] It was, moreover, in the annual Bach festivals at Moravian College and Seminary in Bethlehem, Pennsylvania, that many Americans received their first introduction to the great choral masterpieces of Bach.

According to Bach's Orthodox Lutheran librettist, Erdmann Neumeister, of whom we spoke in the preceding chapter, Zinzendorf was, quite simply, "the apostle of Satan," who had "brought forward for his misled and unfortunate followers" the "damnable doctrines" of extreme Pietism.[3] In September 1721, Zinzendorf wrote the hymn "Seelenbräutigam, O du Gottes-Lamm." It is set to the melody of an earlier hymn with which it is often confused, written by the Lutheran Pietist Adam Drese, Kapellmeister at Arnstadt in the late seventeenth century and thus, in a sense, a predecessor of Bach.[4] Drese's "Seelenbräutigam, Jesus, Gottes Lamm" was first published in 1697, but it has been almost completely eclipsed by Zinzendorf's version.[5] And the melody of Drese's, now Zinzendorf's, hymn is wedded to yet another of Zinzendorf's adaptations of the same material, "Jesu geh' voran [Jesus, still lead on]" (*LBW* 341), which in various languages became a great favorite as a processional hymn for Lutheran catechumens to sing at their confirmation.

Thus, although it is not possible to carry out anything like a precise statistical analysis, it is probably accurate to guess that most of Bach's theological and clerical contemporaries would not be classified as either consistent Pietists or thorough Rationalists or unambiguously Orthodox, but nevertheless as having been affected in some significant way by Pietism, while it is also accurate to declare that "Bach and the church, or for that matter the theology, with which he dealt, were not Pietistic."[6] Any effort to locate Bach among the theologians of the eighteenth century must begin with that statistical assumption. All the attempts by Orthodox Lutheran confessionalists, in his time or in ours, to lay claim to Bach as a member of their theological party will shatter on the texts of the cantatas and the *Passions,* many (though by no means all) of which are permeated by the spirit of Pietism. Above all, the recitatives and arias for individual voices (which he seems to have been willing to use), as distinct from the sections for chorus, ring all the changes and sound all the themes of eighteenth-century Pietism: all the intense subjectivity, the moral earnestness, and the rococo metaphors of Pietist homiletics, devotion, and verse. Undoubtedly Bach was duly grateful to Erdmann Neumeister for his support (including his unsuccessful endorsement of Bach for the position of organist at Hamburg) and for his collaboration, but the gratitude did not involve an exclusive loyalty oath or a refusal to collaborate with other librettists who belonged to the camp of Neumeister's enemy, the Pietists. Yet it would be, if anything, an even more uncritical oversimplification to interpret Bach as a party-line Lutheran Pietist, for he repeatedly showed, by his revisions and by his musical settings of those very texts, that he was not to be confined by the categories of Pietism any more than he was by those of Rationalism and Confessional Orthodoxy.

The most recent general discussion of Pietism in English has characterized its program, on the basis of Spener, as

> a renewed emphasis on biblical preaching and on the experience of repentance and the new birth, the establishment of conventicles for the mutual edification and admonition of "reborn" believers, and a reform of pastoral training that would place less emphasis on scholastic polemical theology and more on the development of a sensitized ministry concerned with the practical devotional and moral life of parishioners.[7]

But if one were pressed for one formula that could serve as an epitome of the entire philosophy, program, and mission of Protestant Pietism in the seventeenth and eighteenth centuries, the best choice would probably be the title of a book that was published in 1728, during Bach's Leipzig years, but not in Leipzig or in Halle or on the Continent at all: *A Serious Call to a Devout and Holy Life*, written by William Law and published in London, has, according to one account, "probably had more influence than any other post-Reformation spiritual book except *The Pilgrim's Progress*."[8] *A Serious Call to a Devout and Holy Life* would have been an apt title for the little book that did announce the program of German Lutheran Pietism, the *Pia Desideria* of Philip Jacob Spener published in 1675, thus exactly ten years before Bach was born.[9]

Without denying, at least in principle, the central confessional affirmations of Lutheran dogmatics, Spener's *Pia Desideria* and the many books that followed it urged that it was time to issue a serious call to a devout and holy life. Each of the classes of Protestant Germany, whether clerical or noble or lay, had fallen into attitudes of neglect toward the word of God and of indifference toward its moral imperatives. Obviously, nobody was in favor of immorality. But the way the clergy were being trained at the universities laid too much emphasis on their ability to engage in theological controversies, at the cost of their ability to engage their hearers in a serious confrontation with the earnestness of the Christian message; for they had to be made to "realize that they must die unto the world and live as individuals who are to become examples to their flock."[10] Worship had become excessively intellectualistic and formal, but "it is by no means enough to have knowledge of the Christian faith, for Christianity consists rather of practice."[11]

That fundamental accent of Pietism found its way into Bach's music by two distinct but not separate channels: Pietistic poems and hymns themselves, and those products of pre-Pietist hymnody in which the Pietist earnestness about a devout and holy life had already been prominent. There are many good examples of the first especially among the sacred arias contained in the so-called Schemelli *Musicalisches Gesang-Buch* published at Leipzig in 1736, which included a mixture of Pietist hymns and orthodox Lutheran chorales. Its place in Bach's lifework is somewhat ambiguous. Philipp Spitta and other Bach scholars of the nineteenth century felt comfortable in assigning much of the content of the Schemelli collection to Bach, because they believed that Bach had placed his own manuscript copy of chorales at the disposal of the publishers,[12] but, as Arnold Schering says, "that is hard to believe";[13] more recent research has made it necessary to be considerably more cautious about such ascriptions. Yet Bach definitely did have a part in the production of the hymnbook, though probably not as large a part as the preface and the publisher's catalogue suggested, and at least three of the melodies are his own: "Dir, dir, Jehova, will ich singen" (*BWV* 452); "Vergiss mein nicht" (*BWV* 505); and "Komm, süsser Tod, komm, sel'ge Ruh" (*BWV* 478). The Schemelli *Gesang-Buch* contained, for example, "Es kostet viel, ein Christ zu sein" (*BWV* 459), one of the hymns of Christian Friedrich Richter (1676–1711), a physician and a close associate of Francke at Halle, which appeared in Pietist and Moravian hymnals, including various editions of the *Gesangbuch* of Johann A. Freylinghausen. In it Richter graphically reminded worshipers of what Dietrich Bonhoeffer in the twentieth century was to call "the cost of discipleship" and the dangers of "cheap grace"—both of these favorite topics of Pietist hymns and sermons.

For the second genre, the older hymn that had anticipated much of Pietism, we have two settings by Bach (*BWV* 398 and 399) of the seventeenth-century chorale "O Gott, du frommer Gott" written in 1630 by Johann Heermann. Heermann is probably most familiar to those who know the music of Bach from Bach's use of stanzas from his "Herzliebster Jesu, was hast du verbrochen? [Beloved Jesus, what law hast thou broken?]" as the first chorale proper both in the *Saint John Passion* and in the *Saint Matthew Passion*.[14] But the eight stanzas of "O Gott, du frommer Gott" also deserve notice. Whether in the original German or in the unabridged English version (now, alas, unavailable) of the translation by Catherine Winkworth, "O God, Thou faithful God" (*TLH* 395), all the best of pre-Pietist Lutheran piety was speaking here, as the believer begged to be able to fulfill his calling here on earth, to speak and find good counsel, to accept wealth, honor, and long life if they should come but to bear his cross patiently if they did not, and to find a final resting place "within a Christian grave." Although the word "fromm" in its opening line refers to God and is therefore appropriately translated "faithful" as an attribute of God, the rest of the hymn in fact deals with the meaning of "fromm" as "pious" (or, perhaps better, "devout"), an attribute of the Christian life.

The piety of Bach needs to be viewed in the setting of these several elements, as they interacted in the church life, the theology, and the hymnody (including the texts prepared by his librettists) of the first half of the eighteenth century. The structure of his piety has been trenchantly summarized by Joseph Sittler.[15] Putting Bach into contrast with the present, which he calls "a time whose Christian inheritance is so pale that it can play both *Parsifal* and the *St. Matthew Passion* on Good Friday and perceive no opposition in content," Sittler ascribes to Bach "not an amorphous spirituality without intelligible content or historic roots, but a very definite faith that was as vital and palpable for him as the stones of the Church of St. Thomas in Leipzig." He therefore feels able to declare:

> I have yet to find in Bach's confessions, either by word or by the implications of his life or in the content of his music, any concern for religion save as that word meant to him the common faith of his people and church and time. The good city of the consummation toward which his soul pressed was not Parnassus but Jerusalem; the songs which drew from him the wondrously sweet and devout arias of the cantatas were not the songs of Pan but the songs of Zion; the spirit whose might he invoked in his labors was not the Goethean spirit of the Cosmos but the *Heiliger Geist* of his stout faith; the river at whose waters he "sings the song of Zion in a strange land" is not the mythological Lethe but historical Babylon.

That analysis of the structure of Bach's piety may also provide the foil for a consideration of specific Pietist leitmotivs as they work their way in and through the texts of the Bach cantatas and *Passions*. They stand in a contrapuntal relation to the various emphases of Reformation, Rationalism, and Orthodoxy with which the three preceding chapters have been dealing.

One trademark of Pietist spirituality that makes its presence felt in the Bach cantatas is the awareness of sin as *Angst*. Awareness of sin had been, to be sure, an indispensable element in Christian devotion and spirituality from the very beginning; indeed, its place in Christian worship and devotion had provided Augustine with the opportunity to prove that although the Greek church fathers of the early centuries had not always spoken as explicitly about original sin as he was speaking now, they had presupposed it by the way they prayed for forgiveness.[16] And the Reformation had concentrated on the sense of sin—experientially in the struggles for forgiveness and faith that had brought Luther to the point of despair and then to the experience of grace, but also theologically in the insistence that there could be no valid appreciation of divine grace unless it were accompanied, and in fact preceded, by a recognition of one's sinful state.[17]

Yet the Pietist cultivation of anxiety over one's sinful state was, somehow, different in quality from what it had been before. One difference should probably be seen in the "sins" that aroused the anxiety. Gross acts of sexual license were condemned universally; but Pietists attacked lascivious mixed dancing, then mixed dancing on Sundays, then mixed dancing altogether. "Games and other pastimes such as dancing, jumping, and so forth," wrote August Hermann Francke in 1689, "arise from an improper and empty manner of life, and common and unchaste postures in speech are associated with them."[18] Ever since the ancient church, there had been attacks by Christians on the theater, both because of its connection with worship of the pagan gods and because of its association with prostitution and loose morals.[19] As a result of this antipathy to the theater, Christian apologists had made surprisingly little use of Greek tragedy in their explanations of the theology of the cross, for that would have seemed to condone the evils inherent in classical drama. But Pietist moralists singled out Christian attendance at the theater as a special symptom of the worldliness infecting the church and made it a sinful act in itself, not merely an "adiaphoron," a morally indifferent act that could become sinful if it crossed the borderland between right and wrong. An epitome of the Pietist attitude toward these "sins," as this was imported into the United States, was C. F. W. Walther's book, *Dancing and Attending the Theater.*[20]

But Walther's more important volume, *The Proper Distinction Between the Law and the Gospel,* illustrates subtler aspects of the Pietist cultivation of the sense of sin.[21] For it presents itself as an exposition not of Pietism at all but of Reformation teaching, and it attacks the Pietists for misinterpreting Luther's views, for they were "guilty before others of this serious confusion of Law and Gospel . . . by making a false distinction between spiritual awakening and conversion."[22] Without quarreling about labels, however, it is possible to discern in such a discussion of sin as Walther's a distinctive accent not only on the sins for which the Christian must repent but on the methods for producing the experience of repentance itself. What makes this emphasis on method distinctive is not easy to specify, but perhaps it can be identified this way: the consciousness of sin that underlay Luther's *Anfechtung* accompanied and even haunted him all his life, and it did not need to be induced; but Pietism—and that includes Walther's anti-Pietistic *Law and Gospel*— sought to cultivate a methodology of preaching and devotion by which that consciousness of sin could be aroused if it had become sluggish, as it often did. In that methodology there was a major role for Pietist hymnody, in which the contemplation of the sufferings of Christ by the individual Christian heart was intended to reawaken the awareness of sin as the debt for which so horrendous a price had been exacted.

One of Bach's early—that is, pre-Leipzig—cantatas (*BWV* 12) is a particularly fine example of Pietist introspection: "Weinen, Klagen, Sorgen, Zagen [Weeping, wailing, grieving, fearing]" (Ambrose, *Cantatas* 48–50). Like the Romanticism with which it displays so many other affinities, Pietism believed in the redemptive power of tears, and from its opening chorus this cantata, whose words were probably written by Salomo Franck (not to be classified as Pietistic), spoke from the heart, and *for* the heart, in evoking godly sorrow.

As a recent analysis has demonstrated on the basis of the pseudo-Ciceronian *Rhetorica ad Herennium*, both Franck's text and Bach's setting of "Weinen, Klagen, Sorgen, Zagen" manifest a considerable knowledge of ancient classical rhetoric in the way they address themselves to the *affectus*, the will and emotions, of the devout hearer, combining the capacities of poetry and music to achieve the desired rhetorical result.[23]

Pietist spirituality and hymnody were well aware, however, that even the redemptive power of tears must have its limits. Therefore the contemplation of the sufferings of Christ both presupposed the tears and went beyond them. Perhaps nowhere in the Pietist religious poetry of the eighteenth century—and almost certainly nowhere in the religious music of the eighteenth century—is the subtlety of that interrelation between the subjectivity of tears and the contemplation of the suffering Christ handled with more exquisite sensitivity than in the alto recitative and aria in the *Matthew Passion*, "Erbarmet":

> Erweichet euch der Seelenschmerz,
> Der Anblick solches Jammers nicht?
> Ach ja, ihr habt ein Herz,
> Das muss der Märtersäule gleich
> Und noch viel härter sein.
> Erbarmet euch, haltet ein!
>
> Können Tränen meiner Wangen nicht erlangen,
> O, so nehmt mein Herz hinein!
> Aber lasst es bei den Fluten,
> Wenn die Wunden milde bluten
> Auch die Opferschale sein.
>
> [It should more gentle thoughts impart,
> To see such anguish meekly borne.
> But no, with you the heart
> From sweet compassion turns with scorn,
> And all unyielding stands.
> Have pity, stay your hands!
>
> If my tears be unavailing, vain my wailing,
> Take the very heart of me.
> That my heart, tho' fails my pleading,
> When the sacred wounds are bleeding,
> May a very chalice be.]

Once again, however, it would be far too hasty to conclude even from such profound affinities between the Pietist cultivation of the *Angst* of sin and Bach's expression of it that Bach was at heart a Pietist. For, simply to mention the most obvious and irrefutable evidence to the contrary, there is every indication, both in the documents of his biography and in the corpus of his musical compositions, that Bach shared none of Pietism's niggling prudery about "frivolous pleasures." It would be impossible to square such an attitude with all the "Allemanden, Couranten, Sarabanden, Giguen, Menuetten, und anderen Galanterien" that comprise part 1 of the *Clavier-Übung*. It hardly sounds pietistic when Bach, in the rollicking celebration of earthy pleasures and country pastimes making up the Peasant Cantata, "Mer hahn en neue Oberkeet" (*BWV* 212) (his last secular cantata, presented as a "cantata burlesque" on 30 August 1742), has the bass exclaim, "Wie schön ein bisschen Dahlen schmeckt! [How good a bit of smooching tastes!]" and do so in an echo of the folk song that says:

> With you and me in the feather bed,
> With you and me in the hay,
> No feather would poke us,
> No flea would bite us.

In general, then, the narrow spirit of Pietism appears incompatible with the large body of Bach's "secular" compositions, to which we shall be turning again later.[24]

As the passage just quoted from the *Matthew Passion* shows, Pietist spirituality had, by the time of Bach, acquired an increasingly distinctive tone in its description of the relation between the individual soul and Jesus. At least initially, Pietism was not proposing any fundamental revisions in the orthodox doctrine that the person of Christ consisted of the divine and the human natures in an indissoluble "hypostatic" union—"without confusion, without change, without division, without separation," as the historic formula of the Council of Chalcedon of 451 had formulated it for the orthodoxy of all time. Nevertheless, the way Pietism came to interpret the relation of the soul to Jesus entailed a shift of emphasis from objective to subjective, from the idea of "Christ *for* us," which had predominated in orthodox interpretations both before and after the Reformation, to a primary interest in "Christ *in* us," which had never been absent from orthodoxy but which had been pronouncedly subordinated to the primary concern with the objectivity of the Gospel history and of the redemptive transaction on the historic cross. Orthodox critics of Pietism pointed to that shift as clear evidence of the heresy and dishonesty in the Pietist program. A study of Pietist vocabulary would certainly show that in both homiletics and hymnody "Jesus" superseded "Christ" or "Jesus Christ" as the most common name, and—perhaps even more significant—that "Savior [*Heiland*]" replaced "Lord [*Herr*]" as his most common title. Even the Pietist theologian Johann Albrecht Bengel, who was almost exactly Bach's contemporary (being born in 1687, two years after Bach, and dying in 1752, also two years after Bach), complained that "by this time the practice of saying 'Savior, Savior [*Heiland, Heiland*]' has become so customary that among many coarse people it is nothing but a proverb."[25]

Because of its stress upon the personal and subjective fellowship of the soul with Jesus, Pietism, especially in its hymnody, developed a predilection for language of intense intimacy, of which the sponsal imagery of Bride and Bridegroom in the patristic and medieval mystical tradition provided the most vivid examples. The accident of language by which, in German, "Seelenbräutigam" rhymed with "Gottes Lamm" made that a couplet which would appear not only in the Drese-Zinzendorf song that Bach set as *BWV* 409 but almost literally countless times within Bach's own lifework and in that of his contemporaries, for example, in the opening double chorus of the *Saint Matthew Passion*.[26] Thus also Dietrich Buxtehude, whose work Bach admired, composed a vocal work (since lost) entitled "Die Hochzeit des Lammes [The wedding feast of the Lamb]."[27] To readers of William Blake it will come as no surprise, however, that the combination of these two images from the Book of Revelation—Jesus as the Lamb of God and Jesus as the Bridegroom—became a rich source for extreme forms of the campaign to substitute "Christ in us" for "Christ for us." The radical Pietist apocalypticist, Johann Wilhelm Petersen, who was born in 1649, a year before Bach, and died in 1727, published in 1701 one of the most radical of the applications of sponsal imagery to the doctrine of the person of Christ, under the same title as Buxtehude's work: *Die Hochzeit des Lammes*. In it Petersen called into question the traditional doctrine of Christ, including the doctrine of salvation, proposing a theory of universal salvation instead. Being himself a talented poet, Petersen lauded the title "Bridegroom" as "the sweetest of all the words attributed to our Savior in Holy Scripture,"[28] and in this and other works, both of verse and of abstract theology, he proclaimed a unity between the soul and the Lamb, between the human race and the Lamb, that appeared to his critics to attribute the incarnation of the divine not only to the one person of Jesus Christ but to all human beings.

Orthodox theologians like Erdmann Neumeister attacked the Jesus religion of Pietism. The passage cited earlier in which Neumeister called Zinzendorf an "apostle of Satan" was a rejection of the idea Neumeister attributed to him, that Christian prayer must not only be addressed in the name of Christ but always be addressed to Christ, not to the Father or to the Holy Spirit. At the same time, Neumeister could write such a hymn as "Jesus nimmt die Sünder an [Jesus sinners doth receive]" (*TLH* 324), which did not refer explicitly either to the Father or to the Holy Spirit but announced that Jesus, as God, offered pardon and peace to all who would heed his call. But he made a point of identifying this "Jesus in us" with the "Jesus for us":

> Now my conscience is at peace,
> From the Law I stand acquitted;
> Christ hath purchased my release
> And my every sin remitted.
> Naught remains my soul to grieve—
> Jesus sinners doth receive. (*TLH* 324.7)

If that were the sole criterion, the retention of the "Jesus for us" even amid attention to the "Jesus in us," it might be possible to see Bach as standing in the succession of such a view of Jesus as that of Neumeister, and no more. But the Jesus arias of the cantatas make such an oversimplification extremely difficult to maintain. For it is a matter of relative emphasis and of distribution across the corpus: the prayers to Jesus cited earlier[29] repeatedly and consistently sound the theme of "Jesus in us," not so much rejecting the "Jesus for us" as often ignoring it. There is, moreover, an affective and emotional treatment of the relation to Jesus that goes beyond the hymnody and the spirituality of either the Reformation or Confessional Orthodoxy.

The cantata "Mein liebster Jesus ist verloren [My precious Jesus now hath vanished]" (Ambrose, *Cantatas* 368–70) for the First Sunday after Epiphany (*BWV* 154) is a singularly touching example of such Jesus piety at its noblest. The basis of the cantata is the story of the twelve-year-old Jesus in the temple (Luke 2:41–52) and the distress of Joseph and Mary over his being lost. That provided Bach's librettist, and then Bach as he composed his solos, with an opportunity for a variety of poetic reflections on what it might mean for Jesus to be "lost." The tenor opens the cantata with the plaintive aria:

> Mein liebster Jesus ist verloren,
> O Wort, das mir Verzweiflung bringt.
>
> [My precious Jesus now hath vanished:
> A word which me despair doth bring.]

And later the alto aria, participating in the despair, pleads with intense feeling: "Jesus, lass dich finden [Jesus, let me find thee]."

Similarly, although the hymn itself comes from the period immediately preceding the rise of Pietism, "Schmücke dich, O liebe Seele [Soul, adorn yourself with gladness]" (*LBW* 224), which Julian calls "perhaps the finest of all German hymns for the Holy Communion,"[30] was especially attractive to the Pietists as well because of its application of the sponsal imagery of Bride and Bridegroom to the reception of communion. Bach takes full advantage of this imagery. In the chorale fantasia on "Schmücke dich," which, as Schweitzer says, "sent Schumann into ecstasy when he heard Mendelssohn play it on the organ,"[31] he demonstrated the potentials of its tonality. But in the cantata (*BWV* 180) that he based on the hymn, "Schmücke dich, O liebe Seele [Deck thyself, O soul beloved]" (Ambrose, *Cantatas* 423–25), an explicit application of the imagery of Bride and Bridegroom, once again in the arias and especially in that for the tenor,

> Ermuntre dich: dein Heiland klopft,
> Ach, öffne bald die Herzenspforte!
>
> [Be lively now: thy Savior knocks,
> Ah, open soon thy spirit's portals!]

made of the soul's reception of Holy Communion an intense and intimate personal experience of union with Jesus that far over-shadowed any of the controversies about the nature of the presence of the body and blood of Christ that had been raging since the early years of the Reformation and even earlier.

A third theme that recurs in Pietist devotion, and in Bach's cantatas and other sacred music, is a preoccupation with death that, in the opinion of some historians of literature and art, was almost an obsession. How an era of history interprets death and related themes may be as valuable a key as we can find to the true spirit of that era. Thus an era like ours, which has made death into the final obscenity—and, so it sometimes appears, the only obscenity—is thereby telling us a great deal about itself: if a comic wants to get a cheap laugh from almost any audience nowadays, all that is needed is to make a wisecrack about death or immortality.

During the century between the end of the Thirty Years' War in 1648 and the death of Bach in 1750, literature and art about death experienced phenomenal growth. That should come as no surprise. Writing in 1906, A. W. Ward estimated that as a consequence of the Thirty Years' War the overall population of the Holy Roman Empire had dropped from sixteen million to less than six million, and that the population loss in some territories had been even more horrendous: 90 percent in the Lower Palatinate, 85 percent in Württemberg, at least 75 percent in all of Bohemia.[32] Refinement of statistical methods during this century has not produced data that are less "soft." Between the Thirty Years' War and Bach's time, moreover, successive waves of plague had devastated German territories. Thus all four horsemen of the Apocalypse had been riding roughshod over the countryside of central and eastern Europe. From studies of how the medieval theme of *danse macabre* was revived in the Renaissance and then again in the seventeenth and eighteenth centuries, both in folk art and in belles-lettres, we can obtain some index of the eager attention that the clinical details of death and dying aroused in readers and hearers.[33]

Christian preaching was, as always, eager—perhaps even a bit too eager—to take advantage of what seemed a God-given opportunity to preach about death and to preach, on the basis of death, about "a serious call to a devout and holy life" while there was still time.

Medieval manuals with such titles as *Ars moriendi* provided the basis in Protestant (and Catholic) Germany for the preparation of books called *Christliche Sterbekunst,* in which the pious reader was to contemplate the prospect of his death and arrange his remaining time accordingly. Once again, it was an Anglican manual, Jeremy Taylor's *The Rule and Exercise of Holy Living* of 1650 and *The Rule and Exercise of Holy Dying* of 1651, that captured the spirit of the time by managing to be serious without becoming morbid. Needless to say, not every manual about how to die turned out as well as Taylor's.

Neither did every hymn and poem. Luther had taken over the medieval poem "Media vita in morte sumus" and in 1524 had produced the German version:

> Mitten wir im Leben sind
> Mit dem Tod umfangen.
>
> [Even as we live each day,
> Death our life embraces.] (*LBW* 350)

Bach in turn developed this into the stately chorale "Mitten wir im Leben sind" (*BWV* 383). But his preoccupation with death went far beyond this poetry from the Middle Ages and the Reformation. Combining itself as it did with Pietist Jesus devotion and with Pietist literary taste regarding such matters, it produced various apostrophes to the limbs and bones of the dead and dying Christ. Theologically and aesthetically, the line between evangelical *affectus* and mawkish sentimentality is hard to draw but easy to cross. At best, such an apostrophe could be genuinely poetic, as in the lovely chorus just before the end of the *Passion according to Saint John*:

> Ruht wohl, ruht wohl, ihr heiligen Gebeine,
> Die ich nun weiter nicht beweine,
> Ruht wohl, und bringt auch mich zur Ruh.
>
> [Rest well, beloved bones, sweetly sleeping,
> That I may cease from further weeping,
> Rest well, and let me, too, rest well.]

But in other places—as, for example, in "Erwäge, erwäge" from the same *Saint John Passion,* where the bleeding back of Christ in its various colors reminds the poet of heaven and the rainbow[34]—the physical qualities of the corpse of Jesus move to the center of the stage.

69

That, at least, could find some justification in the concentration of the Gospels on the details of the suffering and death of Christ. It was more difficult to find biblical warrant for another aspect of Pietist death devotion, the yearning for death itself, which was treated as normal, indeed as normative, for true believers of all ages. Pietist preachers often quoted the words of the apostle Paul, "My desire is to depart and be with Christ, for that is far better" (Phil. 1:23); but, together with the Nunc Dimittis, that is an almost isolated instance of such yearning in the New Testament, and even it is qualified by the next verse, "But to remain in the flesh is more necessary on your account." Yet Pietism developed into a high art the longing for the end of life. Speaking of the cantata (*BWV* 8) "Liebster Gott, wann werd ich sterben? [Dearest God, when will my death be?]" (Ambrose, *Cantatas* 38–40), André Pirro declares: "Never has Bach described the gentleness of death with so much inner ardor as in these pages where the instruments weave arabesques like garlands woven from the foliage adorning the tomb of some youth."[35] Similarly, in the cantata (*BWV* 32) "Liebster Jesu, mein Verlangen [Dearest Jesus, my desiring]" (Ambrose, *Cantatas* 97–99), a duet between Christ and the soul has Christ telling the soul to be scornful of "earthly trash [*Erdentand*]" and seek to fly to Christ's heavenly habitations. The soprano replies with a recitative that reminds many a twentieth-century devotee of Bach of the *German Requiem* of Johannes Brahms, the words of Ps. 84, "Wie lieblich ist doch deine Wohnung [How lovely is, though, this thy dwelling]." In yet another cantata (*BWV* 161), "Komm, du süsse Todesstunde [Come, O death, thou sweetest hour]" (Ambrose, *Cantatas* 381–83), where, as in so many other places, Bach allows the funeral bells to sound,[36] the sponsal imagery of Bride and Bridegroom, referred to earlier, blends with the desire for death, which the honey of the Bridegroom will make sweet—all accompanied on the organ by "O bleeding head and wounded." Thus the Pietist hunger for release from the prison of this life and the Pietist passion for nuptial union with "Jesus in us" have as their counterpart the hymn by which, as we shall see again in a later chapter,[37] the Western church had most eloquently confessed its faith in "Christ for us." But almost certainly the most dearly beloved instance of the hunger for release in the name of Jesus is the one Bach has expressed in one of the melodies for the Schemelli *Gesang-Buch* that scholars are prepared to award to him:

> Komm', süsser Tod,
> Komm, sel'ge Ruh!
>
> [Come, blessed death,
> Come, sweet repose!] (*BWV* 478)

Part II
SOME THEOLOGICAL THEMES

6

Themes and Variations in the Bach *Passions*

The most celebrated large-scale work of sacred music composed during the lifetime of Johann Sebastian Bach—indeed, perhaps the most celebrated large-scale work of sacred music ever composed— was not the work of Johann Sebastian Bach at all, but of another composer also born in 1685. It was, of course, *Messiah* by George Frideric Handel. The story has often been told, in books and even in film, of the inspiration in which he said he wrote *Messiah* at white heat between 22 August and 14 September 1741, and of its premier performance in the music hall on Fishamble Street in Dublin on 13 April 1742. It was likewise in the 1740s (although more precise dating is difficult on the basis of the present state of the documents) that Bach conducted the final revision of his *Passion according to Saint Matthew,* and in the 1740s (probably between 1746 and 1749) that he carried out and conducted the final revision also of his *Passion according to Saint John.*

Thus the present versions of the three works—*Messiah, Saint Matthew,* and *Saint John*—all date from the same decade. What happened to them after that decade depended in part on the later composers into whose hands they fell. It was Handel's *Messiah,* and not either of Bach's *Passions,* that Mozart rearranged and "newly instrumented" less than half a century after its original composition, in March 1789, producing a version (Köchel 572) that modern listeners, accustomed to the conventions of present-day Baroque performance, tend to find rather quaint and slightly disturbing. "There exists," in Alfred Einstein's words, "between Johann Christian Bach and Mozart, to use lightly a term from Leibniz's philosophy, a pre-established harmony, a wondrous kinship of souls."[1] It was not so, however, with Johann Sebastian Bach, from whom Mozart adapted several three-part fugues (Köchel 404a), but no sacred works, although the *Mass in C Minor* (Köchel 427) has been called a "fruit of [Mozart's] study of Bach" and is linked by some Mozart scholars with Bach's *Mass in B Minor*.[2] And, on the other hand, it was, of course, Felix Mendelssohn who reintroduced Bach's *Matthew Passion* to Germany and to Leipzig, setting a style for its performance that prevailed well into the twentieth century.[3]

This is not the place to undertake a comparative evaluation of *Messiah* and the Bach *Passions*. There are certain contemporaries who seem almost to have been born in order to be contrasted: Erasmus and Luther, with their differing experiences of nature and of grace; or Tolstoy and Dostoevsky, who both saw so deeply into the demonic and into the angelic possibilities of humanity but who drew such divergent conclusions from what they saw. Occasionally a point of comparison between Handel and Bach suggests itself from the texts themselves: both *Messiah* and the cantata (*BWV* 21) "Ich hatte viel Bekümmernis [I had so much distress]" (Ambrose, *Cantatas* 68–72) reach a climax in the words of Rev. 5:12: "Worthy is the Lamb that was slain." Any comparison, moreover, should begin by noting that Handel's *Messiah* and the Bach *Passions* do in fact have much in common. For they are all three full-length dramatic treatments of the life of Jesus Christ, based on biblical texts, in which soloists and chorus, accompanied by orchestra, celebrate his meaning for human life and destiny. But within that basic similarity the contrasts are the more striking.

To begin with, as the very titles *Messiah* and *Passion* indicate, the works are not based on the same portions of the Bible. Of the fifty vocal units in *Messiah*, thirty-three, or two-thirds, are taken completely from the Old Testament. Each of those passages had already had a long and checkered history of Christian usage and interpretation, going back in many cases to the New Testament itself, and Handel's interweaving of New Testament and Old Testament passages is so skillful, and so successful, that most listeners probably have no awareness at all of moving back and forth between prophecy and fulfillment. In a *Passion*, on the other hand, the basic text, or *lectio continua*, is supplied primarily (though not exclusively) by just one of the four Gospels, sung by the tenor voice of the Evangelist. The principal characters in the Gospel narrative—above all, Jesus himself—are also portrayed by soloists, though usually (and preferably) most of the minor roles are sung from within the choir. Any references to the Old Testament are more or less incidental, as in the bass recitative of the *Saint Matthew,* which, after the Evangelist has told the story of Joseph of Arimathea, who came to Pilate "at eventide" to ask for the body of Jesus, indulges in this pleasant typology:

> At evening, hour of calm and rest,
> Was Adam's fall made manifest;
> At evening too, the Lord's redeeming love.
> At evening, homeward turned the dove [to Noah's ark];
> An olive-leaf the while she bore.[4]

Indeed, not even the other parts of the New Testament, such as the epistles of Paul, or the other parts of the Gospel apart from the Passion story, play any significant part in the Bach *Passions,* whereas in *Messiah* the one-third that comes from the New Testament is distributed, quite literally, from the Gospel of Matthew to the Book of Revelation.

That far greater specificity of focus in the Bach *Passions* makes them seasonal works in a sense that *Messiah* is not. It would probably come as a surprise to many today to be told that Handel's *Messiah* was not intended for a particular season of the church year, for it would certainly be safe to estimate that by far the most performances of it take place during the Christmas season. Yet its first presentation, after a public rehearsal four days earlier, was on 13 April 1742, which, because England went on observing the "Old Style" (Julian) calendar until 1752, was the Tuesday of Holy Week. During Handel's lifetime there were performances of *Messiah* during Advent in 1750, 1751, 1756, and 1758, but the majority of them fell into the first six months of the calendar year, as had the first. Spanning as it does the life of Jesus from birth to resurrection and ascension, *Messiah* is altogether independent of the church calendar. On the other hand, it has been noted that while "Handel composed music for three churches, Roman Catholic (the Latin psalms), Lutheran (the *Brockes Passion*), and Anglican," his church "music does not show Handel at his most profound."[5] Bach's *Passion according to Saint John* and *Passion according to Saint Matthew,* by contrast, need to be understood in relation to what the introductory chapter of this book has called "the four seasons of Johann Sebastian Bach." It was traditional usage in various parts of Protestant Germany, including Leipzig, to present the Passion story from Saint Matthew's Gospel on Palm Sunday and from Saint John's Gospel on Good Friday. But whether or not that particular usage was strictly observed, the whole atmosphere and musical intentionality of the *Passions* would demand that they be sung during Lent; and that is certainly when most performances of them are still given.

The locus of the Bach *Passions* within the church year belongs to their essentially churchly character, by contrast with the setting of *Messiah,* which, except for performances in the chapel of the Foundling Hospital, was given in church only once during Handel's lifetime, at Bristol Cathedral on 17 August 1758; and that, moreover, appears to have been the only performance of any of Handel's oratorios in a church. In his own lifetime Handel's *Messiah* was attacked for being presented in the profane atmosphere of a theater. Writing under the pseudonym of "Lover of Truth [Philalethes]" a year after the premier performance, a critic declared:

> It cannot be defended as Decent, to use the same Place one Week as a Temple to perform a sacred Oratorio in, and (when sanctify'd by those hallowed Lays) the next as a Stage, to exhibit the Bufoonries of Harlequin.

"Decent" or not, theaters such as Covent Garden and the Academy of Ancient Music in London were the natural habitat for *Messiah.* That may also help to account for the importance that *Messiah* has assumed in the tastes of the musical public, in comparison with the *Passions.* There is certainly enough also in *Messiah* to offend the nonbelieving listener, not to say the listener for whom the Hebrew Bible is the primary Scripture rather than only the first part of Scripture; nevertheless it is far easier to treat it as a concert piece, whose theological content, while never irrelevant to the interpretation, need not get in the way of the performance. With Bach's *Pas-*

sions the situation is quite different. Both the objective basis of the piece, from the Gospels, and the subjective elements, in the arias and chorales, presuppose and seek to achieve an element of engagement in the audience that is appropriate to the church rather than to the concert hall. We are engaged when we hear the conflict between the two mothers in Handel's *Solomon*, as we are when we watch and hear Tosca's struggles to defend her honor and her art. But the engagement does not demand of us that we respond with an existential decision for or against the claims of the story to represent the nature of Ultimate Reality. For that reason, the natural habitat of Bach's *Passions* is still the church.

Because the Bach *Passions* were originally performed in church and, in a sense, still belong in church, their most distinctive musical feature, the chorales, must also be mentioned in any comparison between them and *Messiah*. Bach's use of the chorales in his *Passions*, moreover, sets them apart not only from Handel's *Messiah* but from the Passion tradition itself. Scholars still dispute whether or not the present practice at Leipzig, where the congregation joins in the singing of the chorales during the performances of the *Passions*, obtained there when Bach conducted them. It is an attractive idea, to be sure, but the practicalities of such participation would have been formidable.

Whatever the eventual answer to that question may be, it is far more pertinent to the understanding of the *Passions* to point out that Bach's congregations, even if they did not join in singing the chorales, knew them, and knew them very well. In this respect they differed fundamentally from most of the audiences, at least in America, for whom the Bach *Passions* are presented now. Anglo-Saxon hymnody, whether Anglican or Wesleyan or Free Church, has at various times embodied elements of the German chorale tradition, through Wesley's adaptations or through the translations of Catherine Winkworth (1829-78), a remarkable poet whose renditions of chorales in her *Lyra Germanica*, as Julian has said, "have had more to do with the modern revival of the English use of German hymns than the versions of any other writer."[6] But Bach's audiences traditionally knew almost nothing else and were only beginning to expand their horizons, thanks largely to Pietism. And therefore he was able to weave the chorales into the *Passions* as themes and variations, with the expectation that they would be recognized easily and that their pertinence to the Gospel story would be grasped instantly. Interacting with the chorale preludes for the Sundays and festivals of the church year and with the chorales that formed the climax of the cantatas (as all of these were specified by the hymnals and service books in use), the chorales of the Bach *Passions* become a leitmotiv that cuts horizontally across Bach's sacred music and gives it a special sort of thematic unity.

Yet it is important to remind ourselves that Bach is not Richard Wagner, and that Bach's Jesus Christ is not Siegfried, nor even Parsifal (though Parsifal may well be Wagner's version of Jesus Christ). Thus the Wagnerian term *Leitmotiv,* while all but unavoidable, must be used with care when applied to the chorales of the *Passions.* George Bernard Shaw included a provocative discussion of the term in his book *The Perfect Wagnerite:*

> To be able to follow the music of The Ring, all that is necessary is to become familiar enough with the brief musical phrases out of which it is built to recognize them and attach a certain definite significance to them. . . . There is no difficulty here: every soldier is expected to learn and distinguish between different bugle calls and trumpet calls; and anyone who can do this can learn and distinguish between the representative themes or "leading motives" (Leitmotifs) of The Ring. . . . [T]he chief merit of the thematic structure of The Ring is the mastery with which the dramatic play of the ideas is reflected in the contrapuntal play of the themes. . . . The thematic system gives symphonic interest, reasonableness and unity to the music, enabling the composer to exhaust every aspect and quality of his melodic material, and, in Beethoven's manner, to work miracles of beauty, expression and significance with the briefest phrases. As a set-off against this, it has led Wagner to indulge in repetitions that would be intolerable in a purely dramatic work.[7]

In the *Passions,* Bach actually comes closest to the Wagnerian *Leitmotiv* with his use, in the *Matthew Passion,* of the "halo," the string quartet that plays various chords to accompany each of the sayings of Jesus and, it has been said, "floats round the utterances of Christ like a glory."[8] Heinrich Schütz had employed a similar device in his *Seven Last Words of Christ,* and Bach's friend and colleague Georg Philipp Telemann had also done so in his *Passion according to Saint Mark in B Flat Major.* But Bach was apparently the only one of the three to see that the absolutely appropriate place to suspend the "halo" leitmotiv was at the cry of dereliction, "Eli, Eli, Lama sabachthani," and the translation of the cry (a fourth higher), "My God, my God, why hast thou forsaken me?" The glory of the Father was withdrawn from the solitary figure on the cross: there has been a "halo" for Christ's prediction of the crucifixion at the very beginning of the narrative, and for his prediction of the betrayal, and for every statement of his after that (especially, of course, for his declaration of his sovereignty [Matt. 26:64], "Hereafter you will see the Son of man seated at the right hand of Power, and coming on the clouds of heaven"); but now he is all alone and forsaken.[9]

By contrast, the leitmotivs that are sounded by the chorales within and across the Bach *Passions* are more subtle and more intricate. The first stanza of Johann Heermann's chorale "Herzliebster Jesu, was hast du verbrochen? [O dearest Jesus, what law hast Thou broken?]" (*TLH* 143) figured prominently in the Lenten piety of Lutheran Orthodoxy at Bach's time. For example, the anti-Pietist theologian Johann Friedrich Mayer (1650–1712) made use of it in a sermon "On the Suffering Jesus," published in 1702.[10] Heermann's Lenten hymn provides the first chorale proper in the *Matthew Passion*, while in the *John Passion* that place is taken by the seventh stanza of the same hymn, "O grosse Liebe, o Lieb' ohn' alle Masse [O wondrous love, whose depth no heart hath sounded]."[11] That chorale is heard from again, moreover, in each of the *Passions*. In *Saint Matthew* it is sung by the choir antiphonally with the tenor recitative, "O Schmerz! Hier zittert das gequälte Herz!" and a third time directly after the cry: "Let him be crucified!"[12] And in *Saint John* it provides the melody for the chorale "Ach grosser König, gross zu allen Zeiten."[13]

In some ways an even more intriguing instance of theme and variations is the chorale "O Mensch, bewein' dein' Sünde gross [O man, bewail thy grievous sin]," by Sebaldus Heyden. Sometime during the church year 1713/14 Bach worked it up into a chorale prelude (*BWV* 622). Schweitzer's reading and playing of "O Mensch, bewein' " suggested to him that "at the commencement of this chorale prelude Bach has not attempted to bring out any particular words in the music, since the text offered him none that seemed striking enough for the purpose."[14] But even Schweitzer is obliged to speak of "sighs and groans" in the chorale prelude and to include it among what he calls the "expressive" chorales, namely, "those in which the succession of words, phrases, or ideas is duplicated in the music." It was apparently either from the chorale prelude itself or—as now seems more likely on the basis of what some scholars have recently suggested—from a setting of the Passion story that dates back to his years in Weimar (from 1708 to 1717) that Bach drew a version of the chorale "O Mensch, bewein,'" which he incorporated into the revision in 1725 of the *Passion according to Saint John*, where it became the opening chorus. For reasons to be discussed later,[15] it does not fit the *Saint John Passion* as well as it does the *Saint Matthew*, and it passed over into the *Saint Matthew*; in the process it underwent extensive elaboration, becoming, in Spitta's phrase, "a chorale fantasia on the grandest scale and of the richest style . . . [a] mighty movement, saturated with the most intensified feeling of the divine Passion."[16] Thus it is now the closing chorale of Part I of the *Saint Matthew Passion*, in some ways overshadowing by its monumental structure both the opening chorus and the closing chorus of the work:

> O Mensch, bewein' dein Sünde gross,
> Darum Christus sein's Vaters Schoss
> Äussert und kam auf Erden. . . .

> Den Toten er das Leben gab
> Und legt dabei all' Krankheit ab,
> Bis sich die Zeit herdrange,
> Dass er für uns geopfert wurd,
> Trug unsrer Sünden schwere Burd
> Wohl an dem Kreuze lange.

> [O man, bewail thy grievous sin,
> The Son of God, thy good to win,
> From Heaven itself descended. . . .

> He came new life and hope to give
> That henceforth man to Him should live,
> To perfect freedom rising.
> And shall the Son of God sustain
> The weight of all our guilt in vain,
> Mankind His Cross despising?]

Yet it would surely be an almost universal consensus that of all the instances of themes and variations in the Bach *Passions* the most intriguing musically, as well as the most complex theologically, are the six times that the chorale usually called "O Haupt voll Blut und Wunden [O bleeding head and wounded]" is sung in the course of the *Passion according to Saint Matthew*. It had, however, come by a long and circuitous route before arriving there. The earliest printed version of the melody seems to have appeared at Nürnberg in 1601, as the tune for a love song entitled "Mein G'müth ist mir verwirret [My mind is so confused]," in the collection by "the most important renewer of the German *Lied* before 1600,"[17] Hans Leo Haszler (1564–1612), entitled *Lustgarten*. Only a few years later, however, it became the melody for a hymn said to have been written "for the dying" during the pestilence of 1599, "Herzlich thut mich verlangen [My heart is filled with longing]"; and it has been labeled ever since according to that hymn, even though both the German original and Catherine Winkworth's translation are largely unknown today. It is as "Herzlich thut mich verlangen" that the melody appears in an early chorale prelude of Bach (*BWV* 727). From that adaptation to church purposes the melody proved to be useful for several different sets of words by Paul Gerhardt and other hymn writers, several of which also found their way into the choral works of Johann Sebastian Bach.

Thus it could be used as one of the three or four possible melodies for the Advent chorale of Gerhardt written in 1653, "Wie soll ich dich empfangen [O Lord, how shall I meet you?]" (*LBW* 23). And with that melody, rather than with "Valet will ich dir geben," which Bach used for a chorale prelude (*BWV* 415), or with its own "Wie soll ich dich empfangen" by Johann Crüger, Bach employed this Advent chorale to express the yearning of the church and of the individual soul for the coming of Christ, in the first of the cantatas comprising the *Christmas Oratorio* (*BWV* 248):

> Wie soll ich dich empfangen,
> Und wie begegn' ich dir,
> O aller Welt Verlangen,
> O meiner Seelen Zier!

> [O Lord, how shall I meet Thee,
> How welcome Thee aright?
> Thy people long to greet Thee,
> My hope, my heart's delight!]

As noted earlier,[18] Bach used the melody in the cantata (*BWV* 161) "Komm, du süsse Todesstunde [Come, O death, thou sweetest hour]" (Ambrose, *Cantatas* 381–83) to express the longing of the soul for a death sweetened by the death of its Bridegroom on the cross. The melody is also the basis for Gerhardt's twelve-stanza acrostic hymn of 1656 from Luther's translation of Ps. 37:5: "Befiehl du deine Wege [Commit whatever grieves thee]" (*TLH* 520), each stanza of which begins with the next word or two of the psalm verse; this has been called "the most comforting of all the hymns that have resounded on Paulus Gerhardt's golden lyre."[19]

But "of all the hymns that have resounded on Paulus Gerhardt's golden lyre" the most famous is also, thanks to Bach, completely wedded and "tightly unified" with the melody "Herzlich thut mich verlangen."[20] It is, of course, "O Haupt voll Blut und Wunden." In its origins the text is medieval, coming from the Lenten hymn (long ascribed to Bernard of Clairvaux but now attributed by a recent editor to the thirteenth-century Cistercian Arnulf of Louvain) "Salve mundi salutare," each of whose seven sections was addressed to one part of the body of Christ as it hung on the cross: his feet, knees, hands, side, breast, heart, and head. The final section, "Salve caput cruentatum," hails the bleeding head as the apex of the suffering of Christ and, as the title of the entire poem indicates, the climax of the salvation of the world, and it asks Christ to be present in the power of his cross when death draws near:

> Salve caput cruentatum,
> Totum spinis coronatum. . . .
>
> Dum me mori est necesse,
> Noli mihi tunc deesse:
> In tremenda mortis hora
> Veni, Jesu, absque mora
> Tuere me et libera.

["Hail, head, stained with blood, all crowned with thorns. . . . When the moment comes that I must die, do not fail me then. In the dreadful hour of death come, Jesus, without delay to guard me and set me free."][21]

Gerhardt's German hymn is, in the main, a remarkably faithful adaptation of the Latin original. Thus, as Philip Schaff said of it:

This classical hymn has shown an imperishable vitality in passing from the Latin into the German, and from the German into the English, and proclaiming [its message] in three tongues, and in the name of three Confessions—the Catholic, the Lutheran and the Reformed.[22]

It soon became the most beloved Lenten chorale in German Protestantism—especially because Luther neither wrote any Lenten hymns nor adapted any medieval Lenten hymns. So strong a hold did (or does) "O Haupt voll Blut und Wunden" have upon the mainstream of Continental Protestant spirituality that when the advocates of "Neo-Protestantism," one of whose principal spokesmen in the nineteenth century was Albrecht Ritschl (1822–89), attacked the traditional conception of salvation and atonement, their polemical nickname for it was "Blut-und-Wunden-Theologie." Such polemics aside, "O Haupt voll Blut und Wunden," as theme and variations, runs through the *Saint Matthew Passion* with a persistence and a pervasiveness that makes the term "leitmotiv" seem quite fitting.

Yet Bach does not introduce the chorale until he is well into the *Passion*, and when he does, it is not with its first stanza that he begins. Its first occurrence comes after the institution of the Lord's Supper, and the subsequent words of the Evangelist from Matt. 26:30, "When they had sung a hymn [in Luther's German, *Lobgesang*]."[23] As if to supply its own "hymn of praise" in response to the gift of the Sacrament, the chorus intones the fifth stanza of Gerhardt's "O Haupt voll Blut und Wunden," and in four sharps:

> Erkenne mich, mein Hüter,
> Mein Hirte, nimm mich an,
> Von dir, Quell aller Güter,
> Ist mir viel Gut's getan.
> Dein Mund hat mich gelabet
> Mit Milch und süsser Kost,
> Dein Geist hat mich begabet
> Mit mancher Himmelslust.[24]

> [My Shepherd, now receive me;
> My Guardian, own me Thine.
> Great blessings Thou didst give me,
> O Source of gifts divine!
> Thy lips have often fed me
> With words of truth and love,
> Thy Spirit oft hath led me
> To heavenly joys above.] (*TLH* 172.5)

The sixth stanza follows almost immediately,[25] but only after the momentous declaration of Peter that he would never deny his Lord and the Lord's solemn prophecy that he would do so three times.[26] The response of the church and of the pious soul, knowing as if in a Greek tragedy what the outcome of this declaration and of this prophecy would be, is Gerhardt's prayer that it not have to turn out every time as it did in Peter's case; but this time it is in three flats, "a darker key, having a somewhat restrained and cautious effect":[27]

> Ich will hier bei dir stehen;
> Verachte mich doch nicht!
> Von dir will ich nicht gehen
> Wenn dir dein Herze bricht.
>
> [Here I will stand beside Thee,
> From Thee I will not part;
> O Savior, do not chide me!
> When breaks Thy loving heart.] (*TLH* 172.6)

The third time the melody appears as a choral comment on the encounter between Jesus and Pontius Pilate, specifically on the words of the Evangelist (Matt. 27:14), "[Jesus] gave him no answer, not even to a single charge."[28] But this time the comment is not taken from Gerhardt's "O Haupt voll Blut und Wunden," but is the opening stanza of Gerhardt's acrostic "Befiehl du deine Wege," with the same melody presented now in two sharps:

> Befiehl du deine Wege
> Und was dein Herze kränkt,
> Der allertreusten Pflege
> Des, der den Himmel lenkt.
>
> [Commit whatever grieves thee
> Into the gracious hands
> Of Him who never leaves thee,
> Who heaven and earth commands.] (*TLH* 520)

It is important, for an understanding of Bach's total theology of the cross, to note that the melody of the greatest of all Passion chorales is employed in this particular instance to call attention not to the place of the suffering Jesus as the atoning Savior, but to the qualities in the suffering Jesus that he in fact shared with all the martyrs of all the ages: He was steadfast in the faith and, as the New Testament said (1 Pet. 2:23), "trusted to him who judges justly." As we shall see, that did not exhaust the meaning of the cross for the New Testament, for the Christian tradition, or for Bach; but it was an essential part of the meaning of the cross for all of them, and hence a melody established now in the *Passion* as that of "O Haupt voll Blut und Wunden" was the right way to express it.

But it was as "O Haupt voll Blut und Wunden" that the chorale came into the *Passion*, and it was therefore with those precise words that Bach inserted it into the very nadir of the humiliation of the Lord Jesus, in his purple robe of mock royalty and his crown of thorns. This is, moreover, the only time in the *Matthew Passion* that the chorus sings two successive stanzas of the chorale, the first and the second; but this time the chorale stands in the majestic and heartbreaking severity of only one flat:

O Haupt voll Blut und Wunden,
Voll Schmerz und voller Hohn!
O Haupt, zu Spott gebunden
Mit einer Dornenkron'!
O Haupt, sonst schön gezieret
Mit höchster Ehr' und Zier,
Jetzt aber hoch schimpfieret:
Gegrüsset seist du mir!

Du edles Angesichte,
Vor dem sonst schrickt und scheut
Das grosse Weltgerichte,
Wie bist du so gespeit!
Wie bist do so erbleichet.
Wer hat dein Augenlicht,
Dem sonst kein Licht nicht gleichet,
So schändlich zugericht'?[29]

[O bleeding head and wounded,
With grief and shame weighted down,
Now scornfully surrounded
With thorns, Thine only crown.
O sacred head, what glory,
What bliss, till now was Thine!
Yet, tho' despised and gory,
I joy to call Thee mine.]

Yet even that did not exhaust the variations of key, of mood, and of meaning that Bach found for this Lenten theme in his *Saint Matthew Passion*. For at the Evangelist's words (Matt. 27:50), "Aber Jesus schrie abermal laut, und verschied [And Jesus cried again with a loud voice and yielded up his spirit]," the chorale returns one final time, in the ultimate simplicity of no sharps, no flats, and in a combination of thankfulness for the redemption with personal preparation for the hour of death, with words that have been the deathbed prayer of thousands of pious hearts since Paul Gerhardt:

> Wenn ich einmal soll scheiden,
> So scheide nicht von mir!
> Wenn ich den Tod soll leiden,
> So tritt du dann herfür!
> Wenn mir am allerbängsten
> Wird um das Herze sein,
> So reiss' mich aus den Ängsten
> Kraft deiner Angst und Pein![30]

> [My Savior, be Thou near me
> When death is at my door;
> Then let Thy presence cheer me,
> Forsake me nevermore!
> When soul and body languish,
> Oh, leave me not alone,
> But take away mine anguish
> By virtue of Thine own!] (*TLH* 172.9)

Anyone who has listened carefully and repeatedly to the *Saint Matthew Passion*, especially with a score in hand and a lifetime of memories of the chorales, must surely feel at this stage that Bach has exhausted all the possibilities, musical as well as theological, in this Lenten motif. While in other works, for example in the twenty-one variations of the Passacaglia and Fugue in C minor for organ (*BWV* 582), Bach made each variation more brilliant than the preceding, here he moved to greater austerity each time, modulating down to the sigh of a final Nunc Dimittis and down from four sharps to three flats to two sharps to one flat to no key signature at all as we contemplate the *mysterium tremendum* of the death of Christ. Where could he possibly go from there? One way was to go from Nunc Dimittis to Gloria in excelsis, and from the death *of* Christ to life *in* Christ; and to do that he would have to invent yet one more modulation—to D major, which was the key of the Fifth *Brandenburg Concerto* (*BWV* 1050) and of the "Gloria in excelsis" of the *Mass in B Minor* and was to be (though even Bach could not have known it) the key of the "Ode to Joy [*An die Freude*]" at the conclusion of Beethoven's *Ninth Symphony*. That is what he did in yet another variation of the theme "Herzlich tut mich verlangen," the closing chorus of the *Christmas Oratorio* (*BWV* 248), "Nun seid ihr wohl gerochen [Now are ye well avenged]."[31]

7

"Meditation on Human Redemption" in the *Saint Matthew Passion*

One of Bach's contemporaries was a theologian whom almost any present-day student either of divinity or, for that matter, of the intellectual history of the Enlightenment would recognize, thanks to the prominence of his name in Albert Schweitzer's *Quest of the Historical Jesus* (whose first chapter is devoted to him), although he had done his most important thinking and writing in total secrecy: Hermann Samuel Reimarus. He was born in 1694, nine years after Bach, and died in 1768, eighteen years after Bach. As a recent study of him has suggested: "To his contemporaries Reimarus appeared quite different from the way he appears to us today. There was a public and a private Reimarus."[1] For the public Reimarus was a defender of what he called in the best known of his works, originally published in 1754, *The Principal Teachings of the Christian Religion*. But the private Reimarus had been, all along, working on a massive book entitled *Apologia for the Rational Worshipers of God*, which was a radical attack on most of those "principal teachings of the Christian religion" in the name of a thoroughgoing rationalism and deism. The content of that book remained unknown until some years after the author's death, when Gotthold Ephraim Lessing published seven major excerpts from it between 1774 and 1778, without, however, giving the author's name (which seems to have been uncertain into the nineteenth century). The last of these installments bore the title *The Intention of Jesus and of His Disciples*, and it is this section that interests us here.

For this is how Reimarus summarizes the story of the Passion of Jesus principally from the Gospel of Matthew:

> When Jesus saw that the people did not shout "Hosanna to the son of David" as enthusiastically as did the disciples, but rather that they forsook him, he abstained from showing himself in the temple. He had not the courage to celebrate the Passover festival in the right manner. . . . He began to quiver and to quake when he saw that his adventure might cost him his life. Judas betrayed his hiding-place, and pointed out his person. He was taken the night before the fourteenth Nisan, and after a short trial was crucified, before the slaughtering of the Passover lambs in the temple had begun. He ended his life with the words, *"Eli, Eli, lama sabachthani? My God, my God, why hast thou forsaken me?"* [Matt. 27:46]—a confession which can hardly be otherwise interpreted than that God had not helped him to carry out his intention and attain his object as he had hoped he would have done. *It was then clearly not the intention or the object of Jesus to suffer and to die,* but to build up a worldly kingdom, and to deliver the Israelites from bondage. It was in this that God had forsaken him, it was in this that his hopes had been frustrated.[2]

By total contrast, Bach in his version of Matthew's Passion story used the dramatic cessation of the "halo" that usually accompanied the sayings of Jesus to interpret the cry of dereliction, "Eli Eli," as the climax of the salvation wrought by the suffering and death of Christ.[3] And while Reimarus claimed that "it was clearly not the intention or the object of Jesus to suffer and to die," Bach saw precisely that intention as "clearly" the object of the entire Passion narrative, indeed of the entire Gospel narrative; and, as if to emphasize the voluntary character of the death of Christ as ultimately the result of his love rather than of human malice, he divides the two references to the cry "Let him be crucified!" in verse 22 and in verse 23 of chapter 27[4] with the soprano recitative, "He has done well for all of us," and the soprano aria, "In love my Savior now is dying":

> Aus Liebe will mein Heiland sterben,
> Von einer Sünde weisz er nichts,
> Dasz das ewige Verderben
> Und die Strafe des Gerichts
> Nicht auf meiner Seele bliebe.[5]
>
> [It is out of love that my Savior intends to die,
> Although of sin and guilt He knows nothing,
> So that my soul should not have to bear

> Everlasting damnation
> And the penalty of divine justice.]

With those words Bach states the argument of his *Passion of Our Lord according to Saint Matthew:* that the Savior Jesus Christ suffered and died because of his love for humanity, in order by his innocent death to satisfy the justice of God, which had been violated by human sin and guilt, and to make it possible for the mercy of God to forgive sin and guilt without further violating divine justice.

The standard formulation of that argument had been the achievement of Anselm of Canterbury (ca. 1033–1109), who is acknowledged to have been one of the most important thinkers in Western Christendom during the eight centuries between the death of Augustine in 430 and the birth of Thomas Aquinas in ca. 1225. Anselm was writing long after the councils of the church had set down the creeds and dogmas by which, to the present day, Christian orthodoxy has been defined for the vast majority of Christendom, Eastern as well as Western. In the seven generally accepted ecumenical councils between the First Council of Nicea in 325 and the Second Council of Nicea in 787, the proper understanding of the person of Jesus Christ—his relation, as Son of God, to the Father and the Holy Spirit within the Holy Trinity; his relation, as true human being, to our common humanity; and the relation between his divine nature and his human nature—had been affirmed and defended in response to a succession of alternative positions, which were, each in its turn, condemned as heresies. In more detail than many modern Christians find comfortable, these definitions of orthodoxy specified what Jesus Christ had to be in order to do what he did as Savior.

But they did not specify, in any comparable detail, just what it was that he had done as Savior. The epitome of orthodoxy, the so-called Nicene Creed, whose basic text was the only truly ecumenical creed accepted "everywhere, always, by all [*ubique, semper, ab omnibus*]," as the classic stipulation of orthodoxy by Vincent of Lérins put it,[6] had much to say about the oneness of nature between the Son of God and the Father: "God of God, light of light, true God of true God, one in being [*homoousios*] with the Father." But when it came to speak about the work of the Son of God as distinct from the person of the Son of God, it contented itself with the declaration that "for the sake of us human beings and for the purpose of our salvation [*propter nos homines et propter salutem nostram*] he descended from heaven and was incarnate by the Holy Spirit from the Virgin Mary and was made man; he was crucified also for us [*pro nobis, hyper hēmōn*] under Pontius Pilate, suffered and was buried." But the Nicene Creed left altogether unspecified just how it was that the incarnation of the Son of God had been "for the sake of us human beings and for the purpose of our salvation," as well as just how it was that his suffering and burial (the death is not mentioned separately, being included in the suffering) had been carried out "for us." That certainly meant "for our benefit," but did it mean as well "on our behalf," or even "in our stead"? It could, but it did not necessarily, mean all of that, and even more. Still, a creed and a series of councils covering four and a half centuries, which made the right doctrine of the person of Christ a nonnegotiable test of orthodoxy, clearly did not, and presumably would not, come up with any similar criterion of orthodoxy about the work of Christ.

Yet it was, after all, the work of Christ that made the person of Christ an issue—not merely theological and metaphysical speculation about how a divine nature and a human nature could exist together in one undivided person, but religious and soteriological concern about how that undivided person had become the Savior of humanity. But the proper setting to confess that soteriological concern was not dogma but liturgy, not even the creed in the context of the liturgy but the worship that climaxed, for both East and West, in the dramatic action of the Mass and that was articulated in the hymns of the church. Above all, the sacrifice of the Mass, which the Protestant Reformers would attack as (in Luther's phrase) a "dragon's tail"[7] or (in Calvin's phrase) a "sacrilege" and a "blasphemy"[8] on the grounds that it diminished the glory of the sacrifice of Christ on Calvary, was, already in the earliest centuries, the primary way of celebrating the sacrifice of Christ on Calvary.[9] By the Middle Ages, the sacrificial understanding of the liturgy of the Eucharist in union with the sacrifice of Christ on Calvary was the universally accepted presupposition of both worship and doctrine.[10] The creed affirmed *that* God became man, but it was the liturgy that affirmed *why* God became man.

Why God Became Man [*Cur deus homo*] is the title of Anselm's most influential theological work, but this must be read alongside a shorter work written a year or so later, *Meditation on Human Redemption*. For while *Why God Became Man* is an elaborately reasoned speculative consideration of human sin and redemption, which was written "Christ being removed from sight [*remoto Christo*], as if there had never been anything known about him,"[11] it does presuppose, as the basis for the speculation, a faith in "the deep matters of the Christian faith," and specifically "faith in our redemption," as Anselm expounded that faith in the devotional and liturgical language of the *Meditation on Human Redemption*.[12] The *Meditation* opened:

> O Christian soul, soul raised up from grievous death, soul redeemed and freed by the blood of God from wretched bondage: arouse your mind, remember your resurrection, contemplate your redemption and liberation. . . . Taste the goodness of your Redeemer, be aflame with love for your Savior.

It was Christ who "has redeemed and freed you by sacrificing His own life." For "God's justice required man's punishment." Therefore "God did not need to secure man's salvation in the way He did; but human nature needed in that way to make satisfaction to God." The forgiveness of sins was "possible only if complete satisfaction has been made." But not just any "satisfaction" would do, only "such that the sinner or someone on his behalf gives to God something of his own which is not owed—something which exceeds everything that is not God." Because "human nature itself did not have this payment and without the required satisfaction human nature could not be reconciled, lest Divine Justice leave a sin unreckoned-with in His kingdom," it was necessary for God in Christ to render the satisfaction, since his life "is more precious than everything that is not God, and it surpasses every debt owed by sinners as a satisfaction." And so, "since payment was made on the cross, our Christ has redeemed us through the cross." Contemplating the mystery of that redemption through the satisfaction of the cross, Anselm admonishes: "Behold, O Christian soul, this is the strength of your salvation, this is what has made possible your freedom, this is the cost of your redemption." And he closes the *Meditation* with the prayer to Christ: "Let Your love seize my whole being; let it possess me completely, because together with the Father and the Holy Spirit You are the only God, blessed forever. Amen."

That liturgical and meditational picture of the death of Christ as an act of redemptive "satisfaction" did not become, in the technical sense of the word "dogma," a dogma of the medieval church, but the Reformation gave it an official and at least quasi-dogmatic status that it had not enjoyed before. For the Protestant Reformers attacked the very idea of the Mass as propitiatory sacrifice, insisting that this status belonged only to the unique and unrepeatable sacrifice of Christ on Good Friday. They likewise rejected the notion of "satisfaction" as this had been evolved in the medieval sacrament of penance, which required that, after due contrition and proper confession, the penitent also make amends for the consequences of sin through satisfaction; already in Luther's *Ninety-five Theses* of 1517 that notion was an object of Protestant polemics. The liturgical reforms of mainstream Protestantism, which represented a wide spectrum from the conservatism of Luther's Latin *Formula of the Mass* to the simplicity of Zwingli's order of Holy Communion at Zurich,[13] were agreed, regardless of what else they retained of medieval worship, in uniformly eliminating those words and actions in the Canon of the Mass that attributed to it a sacrificial significance. Nothing man could do, in the Mass or in penance or in other good works, could add anything to the full and complete "satisfaction" achieved on the cross. In their own positive theology, meanwhile, the Reformers took as the "doctrine by which the church stands or falls [*articulus stantis aut cadentis ecclesiae*]" the doctrine of justification, at the center of which was the New Testament metaphor of God as Judge and of the redemption as a juridical action in which God declared the sinner innocent on the basis of the death of the sinless Christ on the cross.

The net result of all these emphases in Reformation doctrine was that Anselm's definition of redemption as satisfaction through the death of Christ was, if anything, more firmly entrenched in Protestant theology than in Roman Catholic theology.[14] By Bach's time it was the touchstone of authentic orthodoxy. "The most precious doctrine of the satisfaction and merit of our Lord and Savior Jesus Christ," Erdmann Neumeister declared in the preface to a book entitled *Solid Proof that Christ Jesus Has Rendered Satisfaction for Us and Our Sins,* was so fundamental that "without knowledge of it and faith in it we cannot be saved." Indeed, "without it all church and all religion would have to collapse."[15] Therefore he urged later in the book:

> Accordingly, what we read concerning the suffering and death of Christ in the history of the Passion, and what during the present Lenten season we hear about this in sermons—that we must all take as having happened for us and as having been done as an act of satisfaction.[16]

It was well and good, he said elsewhere, "to magnify the mercy of God," but "one must not in the process make his justice less; for one is as great as the other."[17] And the "for us" in biblical language about the death of Christ as satisfaction must mean not only "on our behalf [*hyper*]" but "in our stead [*anti*]."[18] It was only the satisfaction rendered by Christ that made the heavenly Father's forgiveness of sins "possible."[19] That was not only Neumeister's doctrine of the atonement, it was the consensus of Protestant orthodox dogmatics across confessions and denominations at the end of the seventeenth and the beginning of the eighteenth century.[20]

That Anselmic doctrine of redemption as satisfaction rendered through the blood of Christ is a crimson thread that runs through Bach's *Passion according to Saint Matthew* from beginning to end, although we can look only at some of the highlights here.[21] It makes itself prominent in the very opening chorus of the work, "Come, ye daughters." This is a double (more accurately, triple) chorus, inviting the "daughters [of Jerusalem]" to weep, not for Christ, but for themselves and for their children (Luke 23:28) and thus to share in the sorrow and lamentation of the Passion. There is a dialogue between the choruses, with the question "Sehet! Wen? [Look! Who is it?]" and the answer "Den Bräutigam [the Bridegroom]," then the question "Seht ihn! Wie? [Look! What is he like?]" and the familiar rhyming answer "Als wie ein Lamm [He is like a Lamb]." At the second answer there comes (as usually scored now) a third chorus, the children's choir, which provides, in Helmuth Rilling's phrase, "an element of liturgically objectified confession"[22] by singing the traditional Agnus Dei of the liturgy in German, "O Lamm Gottes [Lamb of God]." But the German version, on which Bach had composed at least two chorale preludes (*BWV* 618, 656), specifies what the Latin had not made explicit (though it had of course presupposed it): Christ is "Lamm Gottes *unschuldig* [the *innocent* Lamb of God]." And meanwhile the dialogue of the double adult chorus continues with its questions, asking in effect, *Cur deus homo:*

> Sehet! Was? Seht die Geduld.
> Seht! Wohin? *Auf unsre Schuld.*
> Sehet ihn. Aus Lieb und Huld
> Holz zum Kreuze selber tragen.

> [Look at him! What? Look at his long-suffering.
> Look! What is its final cause? Our guilt.
> Look at him. In love and dedication
> He himself is bearing his cross.]

And the children sing: "All Sünd hast Du ertragen [All sin Thou borest for us]." The innocent Lamb of God—guilty humanity: this is the contrast, and this eventually the mutual exchange, of the *Passion.*

Thus at the pathos of the words of Jesus in Matt. 26:38, "My soul is very sorrowful, even to death," the chorus asks the question from stanza three of Johann Heermann's chorale "Herzliebster Jesu," which was itself based on a *Meditation* attributed—mistakenly, according to present-day scholarship—to Anselm:[23] "Was ist die Ursach aller solcher Plagen? [Whence come these sorrows, whence this mortal anguish?]" And the tenor aria, as if to refute the words of Reimarus quoted earlier, makes clear that the soul of Christ is "sorrowful," not out of disappointment that the heavenly Father has not come to rescue him from danger and death, but because he has come to sense the full burden of the exchange:

> O Schmerz! Hier zittert das gequälte Herz!
> Wie sinkt es hin, wie bleicht sein Angesicht!
> Der Richter führt ihn vor Gericht,
> Da ist kein Trost, kein Helfer nicht.
> Er leidet alle Höllenqualen,
> Er soll für fremden Raub bezahlen.[24]

> [O pain! Here the anguished heart is trembling!
> How he faints, how pale is his face!
> The [eternal] Judge is bringing him before the judgment;
> There is no solace, and no helper.
> He is suffering all the tortures of hell,
> Which he is to pay for someone else's crime.]

Antiphonally, meanwhile, the chorus is singing:

> Ach meine Sünden haben dich geschlagen.
> Ich, ach Herr Jesu, habe dies verschuldet,
> Was Du erduldet!
>
> [It is my sins for which Thou, Lord, must languish;
> Yea, all the wrath, the woe, Thou dost inherit,
> This I do merit.] (*TLH* 143.3)

The solitude and dereliction that Christ experiences in Gethsemane, and then on the cross, are the result of the "fremder Raub [alien crime]" whose punishment he is bearing.

That gives not only existential pathos but theological depth and evangelical irony to the consoling final lines of the commentary of the chorale on the words of the prayer of Jesus in Gethsemane (Matt. 26:42), "My Father, if this cannot pass unless I drink it, thy will be done":

> Wer Gott vertraut,
> Fest auf ihn baut,
> Den wird er nicht verlassen.[25]
>
> [Who trusts in Thee
> Shall never be
> By Thine aid forsaken.]

For he who prayed here that the Father's will may be done was in fact the only one ever to be completely forsaken by the presence and aid of the Father, as Bach shows by suspending the "halo" at the cry of dereliction.[26] This orthodox interpretation of the sorrow of Christ and of his sense of being forsaken by the Father as part of his vicarious satisfaction for human sin stands in the greatest possible contrast with the version of the same events by Reimarus.

The chorus "O Mensch, bewein' dein Sünde gross [O man, bewail thy grievous sin]," with which, as noted earlier,[27] the first part of the *Matthew Passion* concludes, also summarizes many of these themes.[28] In the words of the hymn quoted by the apostle Paul in the second chapter of Philippians, Christ had "emptied himself" and come to earth solely on account of the "grievous sin" that the hearers are now urged to "bewail." He has been born "for us," a statement that, by itself, would be no more specific than the words of the Nicene Creed discussed earlier. But this chorale is far more specific: "Er wollt' der Mittler werden [He wanted to become the Mediator]," namely, in the formula of the New Testament (1 Tim. 2:5-6), the "one mediator between God and men, the man Christ Jesus, who gave himself as a ransom for all." Thus the miracles of Christ, by which "he gave life to the dead and cured all sickness," were only

> Bis sich die Zeit herdrange,
> Dasz er für uns geopfert wurd,
> Trug uns der Sünden schwere Burd,
> Wohl am dem Kreuze lange.

> [Until the time drew nigh,
> When He should be sacrificed for us:
> He bore the heavy load of our sins for us,
> For such a long time on the cross.]

The deepest consciousness of sin comes from the contemplation of its cost; conversely, only with the full consciousness of sin can the magnitude of the satisfaction be measured.

That dialectic is at work in the classic contrast between the two kinds of consciousness of sin, that which comes upon Peter and that which comes upon Judas. The extreme ornamentation supplied for the words (Matt. 26:75) "And [Peter] went out and wept bitterly," which is almost certainly the most striking in the entire *Matthew Passion*,[29] becomes all the more so when it is remembered a few moments later during the stark simplicity of the Evangelist's words (Matt. 27:5), "And [Judas] went and hanged himself," which Bach sets to a plain, unornamented recitative.[30] Even the bass solo that follows, which describes how "the lost son [*der verlor'ne Sohn*]" throws down the "reward for murder [*Mörderlohn*]," opens with the plaintive cry, "Gebt mir meinen Jesum wieder [Give me back my Jesus]."[31] The psychological, and ultimately theological, mystery of why the same events of the Passion of Christ should have evoked such opposite reactions in Peter his denier and in Judas his betrayer had long troubled students of the Gospels. Thus the Apology of the Augsburg Confession had concluded that "faith makes the difference between the contrition of Judas and that of Peter";[32] but that only moved the mystery back a notch, leaving it unresolved. And that is also how Bach leaves it.

An even more profound, and infinitely more mysterious, contrast is that which stands at the very center of the Anselmic doctrine of redemption: that the innocent should die for the redemption of the guilty. As the *Saint Matthew Passion* nears the climactic hours on the cross, that contrast repeatedly appears. It can be heard in Bach's setting for bass of the unintentionally accurate words of Pontius Pilate (Matt. 27:23), "What evil has he done?" and then of his self-righteous yet orthodox confession (Matt. 27:24 var.), "I am innocent of the blood of this righteous man."[33] Just before the first of these testimonies of Pilate to the innocence of Christ, the chorus has returned yet once more to the chorale "Herzliebster Jesu," emphasizing that the full significance of the innocence of Christ far transcends the capacity of the Roman governor to understand or to control, for all his boast (John 19:10), "Do you not know that I have power to release you, and power to crucify you?" The chorus expresses its amazement:

> Wie wunderbarlich ist doch diese Strafe!
> Der gute Hirte leidet für die Schafe;
> Die Schuld bezahlt der Herre, der Gerechte,
> Für seine Knechte!

> [What punishment so strange is suffered yonder!
> The Shepherd dies for sheep that loved to wander;
> The Master pays the debt His servants owe Him,
> Who would not know him.] (*TLH* 143.4)

Then, on the cross itself, the full impact of the deepest mystery of all in the Passion story makes itself felt: that the Lord and Creator of heaven and earth should be the one to pay the ransom for his sinful creatures. The law of Moses had laid down the rule that "a hanged man is accursed by God" (Deut. 21:23). The apostle Paul quoted this rule to prove that "Christ redeemed us from the curse of the law, having become a curse for us" (Gal. 3:13). Bach's libretto, and his setting of that libretto for alto solo, heightened the paradox still further by combining it with the statement of Paul that the powers of this world had "crucified the Lord of glory" (1 Cor. 2:8). Thus he goes beyond the innocence of the One who is dying for the guilty to the divinity of the One who on the cross takes the curse of God upon himself: "Ach, Golgotha! Unhappy Golgotha! The Lord of glory must perish here in ignominy. The blessing and the salvation of the world here become a curse by being nailed to the cross. The earth and his very breath are to be taken away from the Creator of heaven and earth. Innocence must die here in guilt."[34]

That is why, upon the death of Christ, the final setting of the chorale "O Haupt voll Blut und Wunden," as noted earlier,[35] can connect the death of the believer to the death of Christ and pray in its final lines:

> Wenn mir am allerbängsten
> Wird um das Herze sein,
> So reiss' mich aus den Ängsten
> *Kraft deiner* Angst und Pein![36]
>
> [When soul and body languish,
> Oh, leave me not alone,
> But take away mine anguish
> *By virtue of Thine own!*] (*TLH* 172.9)

For with his death, the satisfaction has been rendered, and "it is finished" (John 19:30); and there is now "an end to the distress [*Mühe*] that our sins have caused him," a conclusion to the "misery [*Not*] that my fall [into sin] has brought upon him."[37]

Read as a dogmatic treatise, the *Matthew Passion* is a defense, against the theories of Reimarus, of the orthodox interpretation of the death of Christ as a voluntary act of satisfaction rendered by Jesus Christ to the justice of God. Whatever some of the avant-garde theologians of Bach's time may have begun to suppose about "the intention of Jesus and of his disciples," Bach seems to have been quite content, in the *Passion of Our Lord according to Saint Matthew*, to work within the schema first systematized by Anselm. But Bach's *Matthew Passion* is not a dogmatic treatise: even its prose is poetry, and it is all set to music of almost unbearable emotional power. Therefore its counterpart in theology, and specifically in the theology of Anselm, is not the rational-apologetic treatise *Why God Became Man*, but the emotional-devotional treatise *Meditation on Human Redemption*. As the history of post-Reformation Protestant orthodoxy had amply demonstrated, the satisfaction theory of the atonement, when it was transposed from devotion to dogmatics, from meditation to systematic theology, created enormous problems: for the doctrine of God, for the portrait of the life of Jesus

Christ, for the interpretation of the Bible. With the elimination of its full liturgical and sacramental context, it did not make sense—or, alternately, it made entirely too much sense, transforming the mystery of the cross into the transaction of a celestial Shylock who demanded his pound of flesh. Bach's *Saint Matthew Passion* rescued "satisfaction" from itself by restoring it to a context in which it could give voice to central and fundamental affirmations of the Christian gospel.

Nevertheless it is noteworthy that in the *Saint Matthew Passion* Bach reached across and over the Reformation to the Middle Ages. "O Haupt voll Blut und Wunden" was a German version of a medieval hymn; "Herzliebster Jesu" was a versification of a medieval meditation; and the doctrine of redemption as satisfaction of the justice of God through the death of the innocent Christ was a medieval doctrine. How far removed much of this is from the Reformation becomes dramatically evident if we consider one omission which, upon being mentioned, becomes obvious: the only explicit reference to the resurrection of Christ in the *Matthew Passion* is in the words of the opponents of Jesus, who recall his having prophesied it;[38] but in the arias and choruses that speak for the believing community, there is none. There is none because there does not have to be any: Anselm's Christ saves by his death, which, by virtue of his being both God and man in one person, renders a satisfaction to God that is both applicable to humanity and universally valid. All that the resurrection adds to the conventional Anselmic view of the redemption as satisfaction is the assurance that, by raising Christ from the dead, God has declared himself satisfied. But for Luther that was not all that the resurrection added, and that was why the satisfaction theory was not enough for him. It was also why he wrote Easter hymns but did not need to write Lenten hymns. That too was part of Bach's doctrine of the atonement, as will become clear next, in our consideration of the *Passion of Our Lord according to Saint John*. But meanwhile we can hear in the *Matthew Passion* how, as a result of the satisfaction theory of the atonement, grief and gratitude can form an exquisite blend in the supreme choral version of Michelangelo's *Pietà*.

8

"Christus Victor" in the *Saint John Passion*

These efforts to locate Bach (as the title of this book has it) "among the theologians" have been concentrating on Lutheran theologians and even on Lutheran composers of sacred music: Erdmann Neumeister was an Orthodox Lutheran theologian and pastor; August Hermann Francke insisted that he was also an orthodox Lutheran (though perhaps with a lowercase "o"); George Frideric Handel came from a Lutheran background, even though he composed church music for several different denominations; even Hermann Samuel Reimarus, whose radical interpretation of the intention of Jesus in relation to his death stands in such contrast with Bach's in the *Passion according to Saint Matthew,* was a Lutheran professor at Hamburg. Such a predominance of Lutheran theologians and churchmen in a book about Bach "among the theologians" makes sense, in the light of Bach's own theology and churchmanship: as noted earlier,[1] he saw himself as a loyal member of the Church of the Augsburg Confession, to whose Confessions he subscribed and on whose chorale tradition he built.

Yet it would be an injustice both to Bach's own work and to the total situation of theology and the church in the first half of the eighteenth century to pay exclusive attention to Lutheranism. Therefore the very first chapter began with Bach's great musical contemporary, Antonio Vivaldi, who was known by the nickname "the red-haired priest." And in the chapter following this one, which will deal with Bach's *Mass in B Minor,* it will once again be Roman Catholic liturgy and theology that will serve as an introduction and foil. It is, however, also necessary to see Bach's work in relation to the Calvinist or Reformed tradition. At Cöthen, where Bach served for six years, from 1717 to 1723, the established confessional religion was Calvinism, and the chapel at the court consequently was Reformed.[2] Bach personally was a communicant member of the Lutheran "Agnuskirche" there, but his official duties at Cöthen were almost completely secular. Except for the cantata "Lobet den Herrn, alle seine Herrscharen [Praise the Lord, all his hosts]" (*BWV* A5), composed for the birthday of Prince Leopold of Anhalt-Cöthen and performed in church on 10 December 1718—of which only the text survives—all of the cantatas that Bach composed during his Cöthen years were secular. Whatever the "staunchness" of Bach's Lutheran confessionalism may in fact have been, it is a gross distortion to describe those years as a time "when he seems to have lost sight of his goal in life."[3] For he does not seem to have found it difficult to live and work in this confessionally anomalous setting, and Albert Schweitzer may well be right when he says that "the six years that he passed in this small capital were the most pleasant in Bach's whole career."[4]

One of the most distinguished of Bach's theological contemporaries standing in the Calvinist or Reformed tradition was Samuel Werenfels of Basel.[5] He was born there in 1657 and died in 1740.[6] Son of the theological professor Peter Werenfels (1627–1703), Samuel Werenfels began his academic career as professor of Greek and then of rhetoric, but eventually he became a professor of theology, holding the chairs of dogmatics, Old Testament, and New Testament simultaneously. His inaugural lectures as he assumed each of those professorships in turn, one entitled "On the Proper Way of Conducting Theological Controversies"[7] and then two on the purpose and methods of biblical interpretation,[8] show him to have been a learned but lucid expositor of Christian doctrine and a committed but irenic spokesman for the Reformed faith. As such, he was intent on finding and formulating the doctrinal consensus between the Reformed and the Lutheran churches, as for example in a set of "Theses on the Grace of Conversion, on Which Protestants Can Come Together."[9]

Werenfels was likewise articulating a doctrinal consensus between Reformed and Lutheran theology, indeed a consensus between both of them and Roman Catholic theology as well, when, in a polemical treatise directed against the Lutheran doctrine of the real presence of the body and blood of Christ in the Eucharist (and against the Roman Catholic doctrine of transubstantiation), he distinguished the state of humiliation in which Jesus Christ had lived on earth and had suffered the defeat of the cross from the state of glorification in which he rose victorious from the grave to live and reign forever. Werenfels affirmed that it was "in the state [of humiliation] that he completely accomplished the work of our redemption, by having been made the sacrificial victim and the propitiation for our sins. It was also in this state [of humiliation] that he cried out, 'It is finished [*Consummatum est*].' "[10] This description of the work of redemption, which as it stands could have been penned by a Roman Catholic or a Lutheran theologian as well as by the Reformed Samuel Werenfels, combined two passages about redemption from the books of the New Testament traditionally attributed to the disciple John: "We have an advocate with the Father, Jesus Christ the righteous: and he is the propitiation for our sins," from the First Epistle of John (2:1–2); and the saying on the cross (usually counted in harmonies of the Gospels as the sixth or seventh of the Seven Words), "It is finished," from the Gospel of John (19:30).

These passages and concepts had been employed throughout the history of Western theology to describe the work of Christ on the cross. The fountainhead for much of that history, Augustine of Hippo, commenting on the word "propitiation" in the Latin translation of the psalms, asked:

> And what is this propitiation, except sacrifice? And what is sacrifice, save that which hath been offered for us? The pouring forth of innocent blood blotted out all the sins of the guilty. . . . Our Priest received from us what He might offer for us: for He received flesh from us, in the flesh itself He was made a victim, He was made a holocaust, He was made a sacrifice.[11]

Because of its insistence, against the Roman Catholic theology of the Mass as sacrifice, that the death of Christ on the cross was the only sacrifice and the perfect sacrifice, Reformation theology had, if anything, intensified that way of reading these two passages from John, "He is the propitiation" and "It is finished."[12]

Thus (to remain with the Reformed tradition after having quoted

Werenfels) John Calvin invoked "It is finished" to argue, in opposition to the sacrificial view of the Mass, that "no further offering remains":

> Christ also signified this by his last words, uttered with his last breath, when he said, "It is finished." We commonly regard the last words of the dying as oracles. Christ, dying, testifies that by his one sacrifice all that pertained to our salvation has been accomplished and fulfilled. Are we to be allowed daily to sew innumerable patches upon such a sacrifice, as if it were imperfect, when he has so clearly commended its perfection?[13]

And a little later in the same book of the *Institutes* Calvin put the matter even more forcefully:

> [The] true sacrifice . . . was finally accomplished in reality by Christ alone; and by him alone, because no other could have done it. And it was done but once, because the effectiveness and force of that one sacrifice accomplished by Christ are eternal, as he testified with his own voice when he said [in the words "It is finished"] that it was done and fulfilled; that is, whatever was necessary to recover the Father's favor, to obtain forgiveness of sins, righteousness, and salvation—all this was performed and completed by that unique sacrifice of his.[14]

There was, then, something of a consensus, at least among Calvinists and Lutherans, that "It is finished" meant the completion of the perfect sacrifice of the cross, by which the justice of God was satisfied and full propitiation obtained.

"It is finished [Es ist vollbracht]" becomes something quite different from that consensus in Bach's commentary on it, *The Passion of Our Lord according to Saint John*.[15] As the alto ponders this word from the cross, the first reaction reflects the interpretation set forth by Samuel Werenfels and John Calvin:

> Es ist vollbracht, es ist vollbracht,
> O Trost für die gekränkten Seelen.
> Die Trauernacht, die Trauernacht
> Lässt mich die letzte Stunde zählen.
>
> [It is fulfilled, it is fulfilled,
> O rest for all afflicted spirits.
> This night of woe, this night of woe,
> The final hour is passing slow before me.]

Then there is a rest and a change of tempo, although the precise specification of this change, as Robert Marshall has said about other aspects of tempo in Bach's choral works, "is not demonstrable."[16] Excitement in the orchestra prepares the audience, but does not quite prepare it, for the second half of the aria:

> Der Held aus Juda siegt mit Macht,
> Und schliesst den Kampf.
> Es ist vollbracht![17]
>
> [Victorious Judah's hero fights
> And ends the strife.
> It is finished!]

The mood has altered, the scene has shifted: from the altar of sacrifice to the arena of conflict, from propitiation to victory. For "the sudden vivace section, with tutti strings, bassoon and continuo, describing Jesus' victory and finishing the fight . . . is one of the most dramatic moments in the whole work."[18]

Despite its affinities with Handel's *Passion according to Saint John*,[19] therefore, Bach has, in his *Passion according to Saint John*, composed a celebration of the theme of "Christus Victor." As noted several times, Luther had not written or even adapted any Lenten hymns. Therefore Paul Gerhardt in "O bleeding head and wounded" had to reach over the Reformation to the Latin Middle Ages, whose poem "Salve caput cruentatum" provided the theme and whose treatise *Cur deus homo* by Anselm of Canterbury provided the theological exposition for an interpretation of the death of Christ on the cross as an atoning sacrifice, by which the justice of God had been satisfied and the mercy of God had been able to forgive sin without violating the moral structure of the universe. Bach's *Saint Matthew Passion* may be seen as the most powerful musical vindication ever composed of that medieval theory. But Bach's *Saint John Passion* is the vindication, no less powerful and moving, of another theory, the theory of "Christus Victor," for which Bach had to reach over Protestant Orthodoxy to Luther, and over the Middle Ages to the Greek church fathers of the early Christian centuries.[20]

Instead of viewing the atonement in Anselmic terms as a divinely initiated action of the human race through Christ "to Godward" (to use an English phrase from the Authorized Version for which there is no real modern equivalent), this theory sees it as an action directed by God through Christ against the enemies of humanity: sin, death, the fallen world, and the devil. These enemies hold mankind in thrall, illegitimately but effectively, until their hold is broken by the cross of Christ. In one version of "Christus Victor," developed for example by Gregory of Nyssa, the devil is seen as a huge fish that has swallowed every human being within reach, until the humanity of Christ is dangled before it. "The Deity was hidden under the veil of our nature," Gregory wrote, "that so, as with ravenous fish, the hook of the Deity might be gulped down along with the bait of flesh."[21] Greedily seizing that tempting bait, the fish is impaled on the hook of Christ's deity and conquered, being forced to surrender its hapless victims. Or mankind is seen as imprisoned under the power of hell, until Christ the Liberator descends into the prison and sets the captives free. Luther, because of his *Anfechtung* over the tyranny of the law, was fond of following the Epistle to the Galatians in portraying the law as such a tyrant, which Christ had to overcome by being "made under the law, to redeem them that were under the law" (Gal. 4:4).[22] He called this "the chief doctrine of the Christian faith" and accused his predecessors and opponents of having "completely obliterated it."[23] In other metaphors, Christ appears as the prototype of Saint George, entering into fierce combat with the dragon and sustaining a mortal wound on the cross, but slaying the dragon forever; as the Lord God had said to the serpent in the Garden of Eden,

> I will put enmity between you and the woman,
> and between your seed and her seed;
> he shall bruise your head,
> and you shall bruise his heel. (Gen. 3:15)

There are infinite permutations of the theme, as the Greek fathers rang the changes of metaphor and imagery to celebrate the triumph of the heroic Christ and his *nikopoios stauros*, the victorious cross.[24]

A central element in this metaphor of redemption is, obviously, the role of the enemies. Ever since primitive religion, perhaps ever since the protoplasm found itself caught between the power of the light and the power of the darkness, some kind of dualism has provided a way of coping with the presence of evil in the world. Biblical monotheism did not resolve the problem, but only complicated it. Thus in 2 Sam. 24:1–2, King David's decision to conduct a census of the people of Israel is attributed to "the anger of the Lord," while in 1 Chron. 21:1, written several centuries later, "Satan stood up against Israel, and incited David to number Israel." The Book of Job is the most profound—and the most puzzling—effort in the Bible to combine a monotheistic faith in the supreme and total sovereignty of God alone with a recognition of the considerable though still limited freedom of Satan to prowl around God's world doing mischief. The difficulties Milton experienced in taking the freedom of Satan seriously without taking it too seriously attest to the complexity of the relation. So does the appearance within the language of the New Testament of such phrases as "the prince of this world" (John 16:11) or even "the god of this world" (2 Cor. 4:4) as titles for the devil. These titles press the power of evil to the very outer limit of faith in the unity of God; and repeatedly, in moments of personal tragedy or social crisis, Christian language and thought have crossed that outer limit and have come up with a full-blown dualism. So it was with Luther, who described the human condition as one of being poised delicately between the two, with the question of which would win always in the balance—in the balance existentially, in the concrete struggles of existence, but not in the balance ultimately, because God was still God and because the power of God in Christ had conquered the powers of evil. That made "Christus Victor" indispensable to Luther's faith.

The theme of "Christus Victor" did not disappear in the Latin Middle Ages, being preserved especially in hymnody and art. Significantly, however, it was the resurrection of Christ rather than his death that tended to be seen as the victory over death, his death being interpreted as sacrifice and satisfaction. Thus in the Easter hymn of Wipo of Burgundy, "Victimae paschali laudes," written less than a century before the *Cur deus homo* of Anselm, Christ on the cross is indeed the "paschal Victim," the Lamb of God who has redeemed the sheep, reconciling the Father to the world. But now at Easter,

> Mors et vita duello
> conflixere mirando,
> dux vitae mortuus
> regnat vivus. . . .
> Scimus Christum surrexisse
> a mortuis vere;
> tu nobis, victor rex, miserere!

[Death and life have contended
In that combat stupendous;
The prince of life, who died,
Reigns immortal. . . .
Christ indeed from death is risen,
Our new life obtaining.
Have mercy, victor King, ever reigning!] (*LBW* 137)

That was the medieval Latin hymn on which Luther based his "Christ lag in Todesbanden [Christ lay in the bonds of death]," which in turn became the basis of Bach's early Easter cantata, written perhaps already in 1708 (*BWV* 4), "Christ lag in Todesbanden [Christ lay to death in bondage]" (Ambrose, *Cantatas* 29–31). In Luther's hymn and Bach's cantata, the "mirabile duellum" of the medieval sequence became a "wunderbarer Streit":

It was a strange and dreadful strife
When life and death contended;
The victory remained with life,
The reign of death was ended.
Holy Scripture plainly says
That death is swallowed up by death,
Its sting is lost forever. (*LBW* 134.2)

It should be noted that the venue of the strange and dreadful strife was, for Luther, not merely the empty tomb but the cross itself; not only Easter, but Good Friday and Easter, is the celebration of the victory. The reconciliation is accomplished; but, in the formula of the New Testament (2 Cor. 5:19), "God was in Christ, reconciling the world unto himself, not imputing their trespasses unto them"— not "Christ was reconciling God to the world," but "God reconciling the world to himself." For this account of the reconciliation, "Christus Victor" seemed to Luther, and presumably to Bach, to be the most appropriate image.

The philosophy of the eighteenth-century Enlightenment, which provides such an important part of the context of Bach's theology,[25] was engaged in a systematic campaign to eliminate the remnants of belief in the demonic from European Christian thought. It had, after all, been that system of belief that had spawned the frenzy over witchcraft and the fanaticism of the persecution of alleged witches. Recent scholars have shown, from both abstract theological treatises and concrete court records of trial proceedings against women accused of witchcraft, that "the ideological struggle of the Reformation and Counter-Reformation . . . had revived the dying witch craze," not dispelling, but in fact intensifying, the belief in witches and its consequences.[26] As part of their campaign to reform the Reformation itself, Enlightenment thinkers such as Joseph Glanvill (1636–80) had been attacking the persecution of witches and the remnants of dualistic thinking that underlay it.[27] They also set out to exorcise Christian piety of the tendency to put the blame for disease and sin on supernatural demonic forces rather than on humanity itself and on conditions that humanity could ameliorate. It is clear from Bach's cantatas that, in this respect as in others, he was out of sympathy with Enlightenment thought; for the human condition he describes there is one that can quite accurately be described as poised between the devil and God. Like Luther, Bach took the devil seriously, and therefore, in his cantatas and above all in the *Saint John Passion,* he found in "Christus Victor" a way of acknowledging the power of evil and the tyranny of death and yet of affirming the sovereignty and the ultimate triumph of God in Christ.

As in the thought of Luther and of the church fathers, "Christus Victor" appears in the *Saint John Passion* in conjunction with other images of the atonement. The sufferings of Christ as he treads the *via dolorosa* or *Märterstrasse* [street of torments] evoke the believer's awareness of contrast: while Jesus was undergoing this, the chorus sings in a verse of "Herzliebster Jesu" and the first chorale of the *Passion,* "I lived with the world in pleasure and delight."[28] Christ is the model whom believers are to imitate in their lives, so that his submission to the will of his Father becomes the basis for the chorus to pray, in the words of Luther's setting of the Lord's Prayer, "Dein Will' gescheh [Thy will be done]."[29] Sin is a rope binding the sinner fast, from which the ropes binding Christ set us free; sin is a disease, for which the wounds of Christ are the only possible cure.[30]

Echoing the language of justice and merit, guilt and satisfaction, which is so predominant throughout the *Saint Matthew Passion,* the chorus prays: "Let me not turn anywhere in death anywhere except to Thee as the one who has made propitiation for me [*der mich versühnt*]. O my beloved Lord, give me only what Thou hast merited [*was du verdient*]."[31] The language of satisfaction had been much more prominent in the so-called Second Version of the *Saint John Passion*, which is dated 1724/25. The chorus that now closes Part I of the *Saint Matthew Passion*, "O Mensch, bewein' dein Sünde gross [O man, bewail thy grievous sin],"[32] opened this presentation.[33] The closing chorus, moreover, is the German Agnus Dei, "Christe, du Lamm Gottes [O Christ, Lamb of God thou]."[34] Both the opening and the closing of this version, therefore, were better suited to the language of sacrifice and satisfaction than to that of "Christus Victor." Although Friedrich Smend regards the replacements as a loss for the *Saint John Passion*,[35] it is possible to affirm, even without claiming that the change to the present opening and closing cho-ruses was exclusively or explicitly for that reason, that these did prove to be more compatible with the predominant themes in the balance of the work.

The *Saint John Passion* also contains, as noted in the chapter on Pietism,[36] some typical Baroque conceits that do not appeal to modern taste, particularly in the bass arioso about plucking fruit from the "wormwood [*Wermut*]" of Christ's suffering and "prim-roses [*Himmelsschlüsselblumen*]" from his thorns, and then in the aforementioned tenor aria, which immediately follows, comparing the cuts and welts on Christ's back after the scourging to the colors of the rainbow.[37] But these more or less conventional "signs of the Passion," celebrated in the poetry and the piety of the church, also take on another appearance in the work of Bach and his poets, for example, in a bass recitative from the cantata (*BWV* 78) "Jesu, der du meine Seele [Jesus, thou who this my spirit]" (Ambrose, *Cantatas* 200–203):

> Die Wunden, Nägel, Kron und Grab,
> Die Schläge, so man dort dem Heiland gab,
> Sind ihm nunmehro Siegeszeichen.
>
> [The wounding, nailing, crown and grave,
> The beating, which were there the Savior giv'n,
> For him are now the signs of triumph.]

And that is just what happens throughout the *Saint John Passion*.

Scholars and listeners have frequently commented on how much more "dramatic" the *Saint John* is than the *Saint Matthew*, but a care-ful listening shows that a principal component of this "dramatic" character is the prominence accorded to the enemies of Christ, not only the enemies in the Gospel narrative (whose part is taken by the chorus, more frequently and more stridently than in *Saint Matthew*)[38] but the enemies traditional to the image of "Christus Victor." This fallen world, in which the sinner can find no aid or counsel ("Bei der Welt ist keine Rat," the tenor sings near the beginning),[39] responds to the death of Christ with cosmic upheavals, as the tenor sings again near the end:

> Mein Herz! indem die ganze Welt
> Bei Jesu Leiden gleichfalls leidet,
> Die Sonne sich in Trauer kleidet,
> Der Vorhang reisst, der Fels zerfällt,
> Die Erde bebt, die Gräber spalten,
> Weil sie den Schöpfer sehn erkalten:
> Was willst du deines Ortes tun?[40]

> [My heart! See, all the world
> Because of Jesus' woe in woe is shrouded,
> The sun in deepest mourning clouded.
> The veil is rent, the rocks are cleft,
> The earth doth quake, graves open flying,
> When the Redeemer they see dying.
> And so for thee, what wilt thou do?]

For hell has its "gates" open to incarcerate the sinner, and this world is a "prison (*Kerker*]," in which mankind lies captive.[41] Death is a tyrant, from whom we need to be "set free [*freigemacht*]," the grave a source of "desperation [*Not*]."[42]

Against these enemies Christ takes the field. It is noteworthy that, alongside the title "Savior [*Heiland*]," which, as noted earlier, was the standard Pietist term for Christ,[43] the poet (or poets) of the *Saint John Passion* put special emphasis on what an influential monograph on New Testament theology has called "christological titles of majesty,"[44] images of sovereignty, power, and victory. The very opening chorus (in the final version) sounds the theme of "the contrast between humiliation and glorification"[45] in its opening words:

> Herr, unser Herrscher,
> Dessen Ruhm in allen Landen herrlich ist,
> Zeig' uns durch deine Passion,
> Dass du, der wahre Gottessohn,
> Zu aller Zeit,
> Auch in der grössten Niedrigkeit,
> Verherrlicht worden bist.

[Lord, Thou our Master,
Thou whose name in all the earth is glorified,
Show us how Thou in pain and woe,
Through which Thou, Son of God, didst go,
At every time wast,
Even in the darkest hour,
Forever glorified.]

The traditional language about the states of humiliation and glorification, which, among many others, Werenfels employed, is here turned upside down: the exaltation does not follow the humiliation, but is made manifest in it. As Charles Sanford Terry notes, "Unlike the opening Chorus of the St. Matthew Passion, there is no note of lamentation here, no bewailing of an imminent tragedy."[46] Reflecting on the confrontation between Jesus and Pilate over the title "King," the chorus, in yet another stanza of "Herzliebster Jesu," hails him as "Ach grosser König, gross zu allen Zeiten [Great King, great throughout the ages],"[47] even though his kingship is rejected in the declaration of the chorus, "We have no king but Caesar," and then is mockingly affirmed in the superscription that Pilate places on the cross.[48]

It is in keeping with this portrait of Christ and with this characterization of the enemies that most of the traditional metaphors of "Christus Victor" appear at crucial points in the *Saint John Passion*. As Christ stands captive before Pilate, who is trying to find a way to set him free, the chorus sings:

Durch dein Gefängnis, Gottes Sohn,
Ist uns die Freiheit kommen,
Dein Kerker ist der Gnadenthron,
Die Freistatt aller Frommen,
Denn gingst du nicht die Knechtschaft ein,
Müsst uns're Knechtschaft ewig sein.[49]

[Our freedom, Son of God, arose
When Thou wast cast in prison;
And from the durance Thou didst choose
Our liberty is risen.
Didst Thou not choose a slave to be,
We all were slaves eternally.]

Like the *Saint Matthew Passion*, the *Saint John Passion* near the end contains a choral apostrophe to the body of the dead Christ, bidding it to "rest well and bring me to rest also [ruht wohl, und bringt auch mich zur Ruh']." But there is this difference in the *Saint John*: Just as the imprisonment of Christ destroys the power of the prison and of the jailer, so the grave of Christ overcomes the power of the grave when hell is vanquished by heaven:

> . . . und bringt auch mich zur Ruh'.
> Das Grab, so euch bestimmet ist,
> und ferner keine Not umschliesst,
> macht mir den Himmel auf,
> Und schliesst die Hölle zu.[50]

> [. . . and bring me to rest also.
> The grave that is prepared for Thee
> And holds no further pain for me,
> Doth open Heav'n to me,
> and close the gates of Hell.]

But the contrast between the two *Passions*, and between the two metaphors for the atonement, becomes most dramatic of all at two other places in the *Saint John*. One of them has been discussed earlier. "It is finished," which, had it appeared in the Gospel of Matthew, would have provided that *Passion* with the occasion to reflect on the death of Christ as the complete and final satisfaction to the offended justice of God for the guilt of sin, becomes, in Bach's *Saint John Passion*, the central cry in what cannot be called anything but a paean of victory.[51] The other comes immediately thereafter. First the Evangelist sings the simple recitative from John 19:30, "And he bowed his head and gave up his spirit,"[52] and then there follows a bass solo with chorus. At the corresponding place in the *Saint Matthew Passion* there is a magnificent song of mourning for the fallen Savior and of gratitude for his life and death. Here in the *Saint John Passion* the bass solo has some of the same quality. But after the very first line of that, the chorus launches into a chorale—from the hymn "Jesu, deine Passion [Jesus, this thy passion]," which also served as the conclusion of the cantata (*BWV* 182) for Palm Sunday and the Feast of the Annunciation of Mary (Ambrose, *Cantatas*, 428–30):

> Jesu, der du warest tot,
> Lebest nun ohn' Ende.

> [Jesu, Thou who once wast dead,
> Livest now forever.]

In the *Saint Matthew*, as mentioned earlier,[53] the only explicit reference to the resurrection of Christ occurs in the words of his enemies as they ask Pilate to seal the grave. But here in the *Saint John Passion* the resurrection is an integral part of the story, for it was through Good Friday (when the *Saint John* was intended to be sung) and Easter, taken together as a single action, that "Christus Victor" had conquered.

It has become customary for theologians to contrast the idea of atonement as satisfaction à la Anselm and the idea of atonement as victory à la Luther and the Greek fathers, usually at the expense of the former. By solemnizing the former in his *Saint Matthew Passion* and celebrating the latter in his *Saint John Passion*, Bach demonstrated once again his refusal to choose from among alternatives that had equally legitimate authority in his tradition. Indeed, he even brought the two images of atonement together in, of all places, his *Christmas Oratorio* (*BWV* 248). For as has been mentioned earlier,[54] he closes the sixth cantata of that work with the musical theme that runs through the *Saint Matthew Passion*, the Lenten chorale, "O Haupt voll Blut und Wunden," but in the key of D major and with trumpets. But the words under which he puts this *Saint Matthew Passion* chorale are "Christus Victor" words, more appropriate to the *Saint John Passion* than to the *Saint Matthew Passion*—and (so, at any rate, it would seem to modern sensibility) more appropriate to the *Saint John Passion* than to the *Christmas Oratorio*:

> Nun seid ihr wohl gerochen
> An eurer Feinde Schar,
> Denn Christus hat zerbrochen
> Was euch zuwider war.
> Tod, Teufel, Sünd' und Hölle
> Sind ganz und gar geschwächt;
> Bei Gott hat seine Stelle
> Das menschliche Geschlecht.

> [Now are ye well avenged
> Upon your enemies,
> For Christ has broken asunder
> All might of adversaries.
> Death, Devil, Sin, and Hellfire
> Are vanquished now for aye;
> In its true place, by God's side
> Now stands the human race.]

9

Aesthetics and Evangelical Catholicity in the *B Minor Mass*

Johann Sebastian Bach died in 1750. It was also in or around 1750 that Franz Josef Haydn, still in his teens, composed his *Missa Brevis*. This was the first of what was to be a series of Masses for various saints' days and other occasions. To list only those that are best known and are still heard, there were: the *Great Organ Mass* of 1766, the *Saint Cecilia Mass* of ca. 1770, the *Saint Nicholas Mass* of 1772, the *Missa Brevis of Saint John of God* of ca. 1775, the *Missa Cellensis* of 1782, the *Mass in Time of War* of 1796, the *Heiligenmesse* of 1797, the *Lord Nelson Mass* of 1798, the *Theresia Mass* of 1799, the *Creation Mass* of 1801, and the *Harmoniemesse* of 1802. Although he himself seems to have lost count of them, so that, as one biographer suggests, "only chance brought [his first Mass, the *Missa Brevis*] back to him" when he was compiling the catalogue of his works,[1] Haydn is customarily credited with having composed sixteen Masses in all. The number would undoubtedly have been far greater had there not been a ban placed on such compositions—from the date of Haydn's *Missa Cellensis*, 1782, to the date of his patriotic *Missa in tempore belli*, 1796—by the Enlightenment monarch of Austria, Joseph II.

Although there is no question that Haydn meant his Masses to be used in the church and for the church, they are, for much of more recent liturgical taste, excessively ornamental and (to use the usual terms) "theatrical" and "operatic." As early as 1824, for example, Anton Friedrich Justus Thibaut commented, in a book entitled *On Purity in Musical Art:*

Thus our more recent masses and other ecclesiastical compositions

116

have degenerated to the extent that they have become purely amorous and emotional and bear the absolute stamp of secular opera and even of that type of opera which is most in demand, that is, downright vulgar opera, in which, to be sure, the crowd feels most at home, and people of quality even more so than the common herd. Even the church music of Mozart and Haydn deserves that reproach, and both masters have even expressed it themselves.[2]

Or, in the words of an eminent medievalist who was also one of the most distinguished Christian aestheticians of the twentieth century, Etienne Gilson, "the masses of Haydn and Mozart are badly suited to the religious purpose of a priest bravely attempting to say mass during their performance. Such music is there for its own sake, and it does not speak to us of God, but of Haydn and Mozart."[3]

But the opening words in that quotation from Gilson read: "Even disregarding such liturgical monstrosities as the Bach and Beethoven masses, or the requiem mass of Berlioz or works of similar dimensions." In such a description of Bach's *Mass in B Minor* (*BWV* 232) as a "liturgical monstrosity," or at any rate as a liturgical anomaly, this Roman Catholic scholar is joined by various of Bach's other interpreters, Protestant no less than Roman Catholic. Denis Arnold speaks of it as "a ragbag . . . an impractical ragbag."[4] Philipp Spitta is obliged to acknowledge that in Bach's composition of the *Mass* "the external suggestion was afforded by the Catholic form of service," but he insists nevertheless that "Bach could not be false to his own Protestant style"; therefore, Spitta argues, "the B minor mass is scarcely less essentially Protestant than the rest of Bach's church music, but its roots strike deeper."[5] Albert Schweitzer, for his part, finds it to be "at once Catholic and Protestant, and in addition as enigmatic and unfathomable as the religious consciousness of its creator."[6] By setting the text of the Latin Mass to music, Bach was in fact participating in a liturgical and musical process begun by Martin Luther himself, who in 1523 had prepared his *Formula missae*. In his introductory remarks Luther expressed his attitude toward the liturgical tradition of the Mass:

We therefore first assert: it is not now nor ever has been our intention to abolish the [Catholic] liturgical service of God [*cultus Dei*] completely, but rather to purify the one that is now in use from the wretched accretions which corrupt it and to point out an Evangelical use.[7]

Luther also believed that it would be a serious mistake "to discontinue the service in the Latin language, because the young are my chief concern." He even went so far as to make the bold suggestion that

> if I could bring it to pass, and Greek and Hebrew were as familiar to us as Latin and had as many fine melodies and songs, we would hold Mass, sing, and read on successive Sundays in all four languages, German, Latin, Greek, and Hebrew. I do not at all agree with those who cling to one language and despise all others.[8]

A Latin Mass by Bach, therefore, must not be seen as some sort of betrayal of the Reformation heritage, nor, for that matter, as a "liturgical monstrosity." Whether or not the term "ragbag" is appropriate, the compositional history of the *B Minor Mass* is certainly long and complex. Bach wrote—and performed—it a few sections at a time, and it is the consensus of biographers and musicologists that he never once conducted or heard it in its entirety during his lifetime. And, as one of them has commented in evident desperation, "What meaning could Bach have attached to the *B Minor Mass* if he did not even consider the possibility of the performance of this work, completed as it was near the end of his life?"[9]

At the same time, it does not seem presumptuous to express some regret that Bach did not also—not instead but also—take up the proposals for a vernacular Mass that are contained in Luther's second liturgical experiment, the *Deutsche Messe* of 1526. In the absence of such a composition by Bach it would not be difficult to assemble one from the *disjecta membra* of his other works, many of them settings of hymns that Luther and others wrote specifically as vernacular counterparts to most of the principal components of the Latin Mass:

1. For the Kyrie, not only BWV 371, "Kyrie, Gott Vater in Ewigkeit [Kyrie, God the eternal Father]," but the two additional settings of that chorale from the Catechism Preludes in part 3 of the *Clavier-Übung,* BWV 669 and 672.

2. For the Gloria, the immediately following preludes from the same series, "Allein Gott in der Höh sei Ehr' [All glory be to God on high]," BWV 675 and 676, together with the fughetta on that chorale, BWV 677, plus chorale prelude BWV 260.

3. For the Credo, Bach's elaboration of Luther's German Credo,

"Wir glauben all' an einen Gott [We all believe in one true God]," *BWV* 437, but especially the version that appears in the Catechism Preludes, *BWV* 680 and its accompanying fughetta, *BWV* 681.

4. For the Sanctus, "Heilig, heilig [Holy, holy]," *BWV* 325 (but of course, despite the title, not related to Reginald Heber's well-known English hymn).

5. For the Agnus Dei, any of the settings of "O Lamm Gottes unschuldig [Lamb of God, pure and holy]," such as *BWV* 401, 618, or 656; or the children's chorus from the opening of the *Saint Matthew Passion*;[10] or *BWV* 619, "Christe, du Lamm Gottes [Christ, thou Lamb of God]."

But a consideration of the Latin Mass that Bach did compose rather than the German Mass that he might have composed reveals the *Mass in B Minor* as the premier example of Bach's relation to the musical and liturgical forms of the preceding centuries. It is, therefore, a case study in "Evangelical Catholicity." This is a term employed by Nathan Söderblom and others in describing the particular means through which the heirs of the Lutheran Reformation sought to affirm central elements of the Catholic tradition that had come down to them from the patristic and medieval periods and simultaneously to give theological and cultural expression to the "rediscovery of the gospel" and the renewal of the church that had come through the events of the sixteenth century.[11] Of the sacred music of Bach, as of the contemporary rococo churches of Bavaria, it may be said that "it occupies the threshold to our own aesthetic culture." Because "the history of art must be understood against the background of the history of ideas and, beyond that, of history," it is as true of Bach's music as it is of Bavarian rococo architecture that "the limits of an approach that neglects the history of ideas become particularly evident when we are dealing with religious art."[12] An examination of the *B Minor Mass* is, consequently, the best possible means of eliciting from Bach's work some of the fundamental aesthetic principles that would seem to have been at work in his compositions for the church—a task that was undertaken, boldly if not always successfully, early in this century by André Pirro.[13] Gilson's analysis of the possibilities and limitations of any so-called Christian aesthetics may likewise serve as a foil for formulating some of those principles in a more systematic way than this primarily historical analysis has done thus far. For, standing though it did in the several continuities examined here (Orthodoxy, Pietism, and Rationalism), the *Mass in B Minor,* more than any of those movements, nevertheless affirmed above all the continuity of the church itself. As one scholar has said, in contrasting both Pietism and Protestant Orthodoxy with the main body of the Christian tradition, "heretofore [in Protestant Orthodoxy] the leaders of the church had forgotten the church or the communion of saints because of pure doctrine; now [in Pietism] they forgot the church in their zeal for a Christian life. They were both unchurchly."[14]

From Bach's practice, as documented in the *Mass,* it does not seem presumptuous to conclude that according to him, the highest activity of the human spirit was the praise of God, but that such praise involved the total activity of the spirit. Bach's setting does not include the Canon of the Mass, which had been the principal object of Luther's criticism. Nor does it contain the Preface of the Mass, in which the celebrant calls out to the people, "Sursum corda! [Lift up your hearts!]" and the people respond, "Habemus ad Dominum! [We have lifted them to the Lord!]" But that theme was represented throughout his sacred music—for example, in his several settings of the Magnificat, whose opening words, "Magnificat anima mea Dominum, et exultavit spiritus meus in Deo Salutari meo [My soul doth magnify the Lord, and my spirit hath rejoiced in God my Savior]," are a biblical parallel, if not a biblical source, for the "Sursum corda." For Bach as for the tradition of the "Sursum corda," therefore, any ultimate object of the uplifted heart short of the Lord himself was unworthy of the best aspirations of a human spirit created and re-created by the "Gott Schöpfer, Heiliger Geist," to whom *BWV 370, BWV 631,* and *BWV 667,* as preludes based on Luther's version of the "Veni, Creator Spiritus,"[15] were all devoted.

The *Mass in B Minor* is a rich source of various doxologies illustrating this principle. The soprano aria "Laudamus te" bespeaks a sense of high and holy privilege in having the opportunity to praise and bless the Almighty. Such a sense does not come through as clearly as it should when the soprano handles the aria as though it were opera, intended to display the virtuosity of the soloist (although such a passage as the phrase "Et benedicimus tibi" certainly provides ample opportunity for virtuosity). There is still need for a comparative analysis of, on the one hand, all of Bach's settings of the "Gloria Patri" (as they appear in various of the cantatas) and of the "Gloria in excelsis" (including the version that appears in Luther's Christmas carol for children, "Vom Himmel hoch da komm' ich her"[16]) and, on the other hand, the massive "Gloria in excelsis" of the *Mass in B Minor*. These settings document the exhilaration of a full-throated praise of God. In spite of the criticisms that his contemporaries and some fastidious hearers since have voiced against it, the same overpowering joy was at work in Bach's three slightly rococo chorale preludes on the macaronic German-Latin Christmas carol "In dulci jubilo" (*BWV* 368, *BWV* 608, and perhaps especially *BWV* 729). The joy also throbs in the cadences of the cantata for 24 June, which is Midsummer Day as well as the Feast of Saint John the Baptist (*BWV* 30), "Freue dich, erlöste Schar [Joyful be, O ransomed throng]" (Ambrose, *Cantatas* 90–93). As Philipp Spitta says, this sacred cantata "is founded on the secular cantata, 'Angenehmes Wiederau' [*BWV* 30a), and expresses a calm and happy feeling which is less suited to the dogmatic character of the festival than to the time of year at which it is held."[17] Such adoration was the most exalted expression of the human spirit.

As the praise of the eternal God, therefore, Christian art was an expression of boundless freedom; but as the praise of the God who had limited himself in the incarnation, it bound itself to form. The conception of art as freedom and release from the bonds of finiteness was an ancient one, found in certain Greek views of the artist as one set apart from the ordinary limitations of human life. Even before Romanticism had elevated this into an article of faith, the soul athirst for the Eternal had found in art the consummation that was denied to it elsewhere. And so Romanticism's quest for the aesthetic absolute runs throughout the history of art. Perhaps no one has described this striving for the absolute in more vital terms than Oswald Spengler in *The Decline of the West*, with his discussion of what he identifies as the "Faustian" element in Western thought. Like Faust, the striving has also been predestined to damnation. Therefore artists have had to content themselves with the realization that they would always be thrown back by the limitations of their finite existence. Thus Richard Wagner defined the artist's task: "In truth the greatness of the poet can be best measured by what he refrains from saying, in order to let the inexpressible speak to us in secrecy."[18]

Artists have had to limit themselves because they were finite and because the matters they described were finite too. But Christian artists have felt able to claim that they were not dealing only with the finite and the temporal. Like Bach, they have stood before the throne of earthly kings; but Bach's last composition, "Vor deinen Thron tret' ich hiermit [And now I step before thy throne]" (*BWV* 668), has become a mythic symbol of how they have also stepped before the eternal throne itself.[19] A Christian artist like Bach was therefore a citizen of the Eternal City, praising a God who was almighty and everlasting. Thus it would seem that he of all artists could be liberated from this finiteness which so easily besets us and be free to soar, unfettered and unbounded, in the timeless and spaceless realms of the absolute. In a sense, it is true that Christian art has been an expression of boundless freedom, for it has been the worship of the eternal God, not of idols. Thus Christian artists have succeeded in creating beauties that seemed to be not of this mortal realm. The antiphons in Bach's setting of the "Sanctus" for the *Mass in B Minor* have seemed to many hearers not only to fill the earth and the heavens with the glory of God, as the words "Pleni sunt coeli et terra gloria ejus [Heaven and earth are full of thy glory]" declare, but to go beyond their periphery into the very presence of the Almighty. Bach's artistry in the *Mass* has indeed bespoken a boundless freedom.

But it has done so by voluntarily binding itself to form.[20] The God whom the *Mass in B Minor* adored was not some Timeless One who lived in endless self-contemplation as the unmoved Prime Mover, but the Holy One who was available within this bounded existence through the boundedness of the historical figure of Jesus Christ. Like all authentically Christian art, Bach's *Mass* concerned itself with the absolute and the Eternal as this had been revealed in Christ. Therefore Bach's soaring version of the "Pleni sunt coeli [Heaven and earth are full of thy glory]" was followed by one of the loveliest and most plaintive of all his tenor arias, "Benedictus qui venit in nomine Domini [Blessed is he who comes in the name of the Lord]," dealing as it did with the one who indeed "came in the name of the Lord," but, as the Gospel for Palm Sunday (Matt. 21:5) made clear, came as one who was lowly and "humble." The canonic duet of soprano and alto in Bach's *Mass*, "Et in unum Dominum [And in one Lord Jesus Christ]," has indeed been interpreted as a musical representation of the orthodox dogma of the Council of Nicea that the Father and the Son were distinct and yet equal.[21] That makes it all the more striking that Bach should follow it with one of his best "step-motifs" in the "Et incarnatus est [And was incarnate by the Holy Spirit of the Virgin Mary]," with the descent of the Infinite into the finiteness of the flesh. Nor was this combination of the boundless freedom of the Eternal with the boundedness of the Incarnate confined to the *Mass in B Minor*. It runs, for example, throughout the *Christmas Oratorio*.

As the medium of a historical faith, therefore, Bach's art had to be cast in the terms set down in the historical repository of its tradition; but as an expression of faith in the living God, it had to be relevant and contemporary in its use of this repository. An outstanding illustration of this principle is Bach's setting of the Nicene Creed in the *Mass*.[22] The so-called Nicene Creed might well be termed the most authentic piece of Christian tradition since the New Testament, in the sense that, despite the designation "the three ecumenical creeds" for the Apostles' Creed, the Nicene Creed, and the Athanasian Creed, it is the only credal formulation that, with one important variation (the notorious Western "Filioque" clause, attributing the procession of the Holy Spirit to both the Father and the Son[23]), has been used liturgically and accepted dogmatically by both Eastern and Western churches. It has been a criterion of orthodoxy for a millennium and a half, and it is still being recited by the faithful and chanted by choirs all over the world and all over the church.

In Bach's own time the Nicene Creed was coming under increasingly heavy fire from the thinkers of the Enlightenment. His radical Pietist contemporary, Johann Konrad Dippel (1673-1734), writing under the pen name "Christianus Democritus," asserted that "through this Council of Nicea . . . [nothing but] great confusion arose among the orthodox."[24] But this was the creed that Bach used in the *Mass in B Minor*, as the order of the Mass prescribed. Opinions vary as to its adaptability. Schweitzer comments:

> The *Symbolum Nicaenum* is a hard nut for a composer to crack. If ever there was a text put together without any idea of its being set to music it is this, in which the Greek theologians have laid down their correct

and dry formulas for the conception of the godhead of Christ. In no Mass has the difficulty of writing music for the *Credo* been so completely overcome as in this of Bach's. He has taken the utmost possible advantage of any dramatic ideas in the text; when emotion can be read into it he does so.[25]

In keeping with his attitude, as expressed in his *The Quest of the Historical Jesus,* toward classical orthodox Christology as the "graveclothes of the dogma of the Dual Nature,"[26] Schweitzer seems to hold, despite the thousands of musical settings of the Mass, that the Nicene Creed with its elaborate second article does not easily lend itself to musical adaptation. John Calvin would appear to have been more accurate in his evaluation of the Nicene Creed: "It is, you see, more a hymn suited for singing than a formula for confession."[27] Schweitzer himself seems to suggest this when he says a little later:

> Bach thus proves that the dogma can be expressed much more clearly and satisfactorily in music than in verbal formulae. His exegesis of these passages in the Nicene Creed has resolved the disputes that excited the Eastern world for many generations and finally delivered it over to Islam; his presentation of the dogma even makes it acceptable and comprehensible to minds for which dogma has no attraction.[28]

This account of the causal connection between Greek Christian theology and the triumph of Islam may be questioned, but Schweitzer's central point must be granted.

It cannot be denied that Bach was an orthodox trinitarian in his theology. There is no reason to believe that he approached the Nicene Creed with the practiced skepticism of the historians of dogma in his own time and in ours, bent upon finding there the traces of the various theological schools and evidences of political compromise between them. The cantata for Trinity Sunday (*BWV* 176), "Es ist ein trotzig und verzagt Ding [There is a daring and a shy thing]" (Ambrose, *Cantatas* 414–16), closes with the lines:

Hoch über alle Götter,
Gott Vater, Sohn und Heilger Geist,
Der Frommen Schutz und Retter,
Ein Wesen, drei Personen.

[All other gods excelling,
God Father, Son and Holy Ghost,

Of good men shield and Savior,
One being, but three persons.]

But he was not only a trinitarian who employed traditional termi-
nology; he was at the same time a trinitarian who sought to restate
the traditional dogma of the Trinity in a manner that was relevant
and contemporary. He bypassed the elements in the Creed that
were the most important to the controversialists who put it
together, such as "consubstantialem [one in being, *homoousios*]" as
a term for the relation of Father and Son, in favor of those elements
that lent themselves to existential reinterpretation. The greatness of
Bach's *Mass* lies in the fact that it managed to take the full measure
of the tradition without losing itself in archaeology.

It does not appear arbitrary to move from this principle to the
conclusion that Bach's sacred music did not have a primarily
programmatic function in relation to the text, but that it could
illuminate or even transcend the content of the words to which it
was joined. Thus it could, for example, illuminate contrasts either
implicit or explicit in the text. One such contrast in Bach's *Mass* is
the transition from the second "Kyrie" to the "Gloria in excelsis,"
where Bach "completely changes his compositional style. He calls
out the trumpets and timpani and exchanges the oboes d'amore for
the more powerfull [*sic*], regular oboes."[29] After the worshiping congregation, speaking through the chorus and soloists, had thrice
begged for forgiving mercy in plaintive assurance, it is moved to
break forth: "Gloria in excelsis Deo! [Glory to God in the highest!]"
The contrast of mood between the closing strains of the "Kyrie" and
the opening bars of the "Gloria" in Bach's version makes the suggestion appropriate that "it is better to interpose a fairly long pause
between them, during which orchestra, choir and audience can
traverse in silence the ground between the *Kyrie* and the *Gloria*, and
ascend from the depths of the minor to the heights of the major
harmonies from which, with the first D major chords, the world of
praise and thanksgiving will be opened out before them."[30]

Another such contrast in Bach's *Mass* comes during the second
article of the "Credo." The setting of the "Crucifixus etiam pro nobis
sub Pontio Pilato, passus et sepultus est [Crucified also for us under
Pontius Pilate, suffered and was buried]" articulates a grief seem-

ingly beyond consolation. Although Bach was indeed willing, in the *Passion according to Saint John*,[31] to introduce the chorale,

> Jesus, thou who once wast dead,
> Livest now forever,

immediately upon the death of Christ, here in the *B Minor Mass* he made the contrast between "passus et sepultus est" and "Et resurrexit" so profound and so brilliant that at performances even today the members of the audience gasp audibly. A similar treatment appears in the third article of the Creed, where Bach expressed a significant contrast that only a few commentators, whether musical or theological, have noted in the Nicene Creed. "Confiteor unum baptisma in remissionem peccatorum [I acknowledge one baptism for the remission of sins]" became an occasion for him to contemplate the reality of sin and the inevitability of death rather than merely an opportunity to rejoice in baptism. And then slowly, as if not too quickly to disturb the penance, the strings and voices moved up to "Expecto resurrectionem mortuorum," which finally tears itself loose from all preoccupation with death and sin in an ecstatic outburst.

This same chorus illustrates another way that Bach illumined the meaning of the text in his *B Minor Mass*, by bringing out implicit relationships between various parts of the text that might otherwise be missed. The melody of "Expecto resurrectionem mortuorum" in the third article of the Creed is a musical echo of the setting of "Et resurrexit" in the second: by raising Christ from the dead, God had granted believers the hope of their resurrection to life eternal. By his setting of the two clauses Bach reminded his hearers that the source of this hope was the resurrection of Christ as the Second Adam, the new Head of the human race. There was a similar echo in the relation between "Gratias agimus" and the closing chorus of the *Mass*, the mighty "Dona nobis pacem." The peace for which this final chorus prayed was that peace which the world could not give, for it was a peace that came only in a life that gave thanks to God—but gave thanks to him for his great glory! And it acknowledged that this peace was a gift from the God who was glorious and lifted up, the God in Christ to whom the bass solo had sung: "Quoniam tu solus sanctus, tu solus Dominus [For thou only art holy, thou only art the Lord]."

In addition to bringing out contrasts and implicit connections in the text of the *Mass*, Bach also illuminated the text by bringing out its full scope and meaning as affirmed by the Catholic tradition. This function of the music comes into evidence in the "Benedictus" and the "Agnus Dei," which Bach managed to relate to his whole conception of the *Mass*. Schweitzer has noted the difference at this point between Bach's *Mass in B Minor* and Beethoven's *Missa Solemnis*:

> For Beethoven, the symphonist, these two sections are the culminating point of the drama of the Mass as he conceives it; for Bach, who thinks in terms of the church, they are the point at which it all dies slowly away. In Beethoven's *Agnus Dei* the cry of the pained and terrified soul for salvation is almost dreadful in its intensity; Bach's *Agnus Dei* is the song of the soul redeemed.[32]

Far from being a "liturgical monstrosity," therefore, Bach's *Mass in B Minor* is a liturgical, theological, and aesthetic celebration of the Evangelical Catholicity that marked his entire lifework. More perhaps than any other of his sacred compositions, it brought together the disparate elements of his thought and work and united them in a sublime unity.

CONCLUSION

10

Johann Sebastian Bach— Between Sacred and Secular

In each of the preceding nine chapters, the place of Johann Sebastian Bach in the musical and theological context of the first half of the eighteenth century has emerged from a comparison and contrast between him and one of his contemporaries—Antonio Vivaldi, August Hermann Francke, George Frideric Handel, Hermann Samuel Reimarus, Samuel Werenfels, Franz Josef Haydn. But for this final contrast and comparison of Bach with his own time, the most striking contemporary contrast is with none of these, but with Johann Sebastian Bach himself. For the issue that any interpretation of Bach's music or of Bach's personality must confront is what Leo Schrade has called "the conflict between the sacred and the secular" in him and in his work.[1] How is that relation to be understood? From what it is possible to conclude on the basis of the documents available, how did Bach himself conceive of that relation? Was he the "staunch Lutheran" of parsonage legend, one for whom the sacred music of the chorales and cantatas was the most authentic expression of his deepest aspirations? Or would it be more accurate to demythologize this legend and to see in him a secular modern man who did what he had to do, or more precisely what he was paid to do, including chorales and church cantatas, but for whom the music was the thing and the text was incidental? Which trilogy explains which: the *Brandenburg Concertos, The Art of the Fugue,* and the *Well-Tempered Clavier*—or the *Saint Matthew Passion,* the *Saint John Passion,* and the *B Minor Mass?*

As such questions make all too obvious, it is easy to caricature both sides in the dispute and, in the process, to trivialize the dispute, indeed, to trivialize Bach himself. Yet a dispute there is. The well-known and eminently convenient collection of primary sources and documents about Bach's life, originally put together in 1945 by Hans T. David and Arthur Mendel, may serve as documentation for the history of this dispute as well as for the history of Bach's life as such. After commenting that the paucity of written sources from Bach himself makes any effort to penetrate into Bach's inner life—or, to use a term that appears to have already been invented by that time but that did not come into common use until more recently, to write a "psychobiography" of Bach—difficult or impossible, because "our knowledge of Bach's personality in action, apart from music-making, is sparse indeed," the authors, in their introductory chapter, "Bach: A Portrait in Outline," made the following observation:

> For the expression of emotion, however, Bach hardly needed to resort to words. *The focus of his emotional life was undoubtedly in religion, and in the service of religion through music.* This would be clear from his work alone, of which music written for church services comprises by far the greater portion—music which, though still the least known, constitutes his greatest effort and achievement. But there is external evidence, too, of his deep interest in religious matters in the extensive list of theological books included in the appraisal of his estate. In the religious controversies of the time, Bach quite naturally ranged himself, although passively, on the side of orthodoxy and against Pietism—a movement that sought an intensification of individual religious experience, and one that was tinged with a certain hostility toward elaborate church music.[2]

The account in the final sentence does not do justice to the complexity of Bach's position within (and in some ways beyond) the conflicts between Orthodoxy and Pietism, or within the conflicts between both of those and the Rationalism of the *Aufklärung,* neither of which can be characterized quite so unequivocally as David and Mendel suggested.[3]

But it is with the main point of their interpretation that recent scholarship has been concerned. For in the forty years since that paragraph was originally published, the validity of their statement that "the focus of his emotional life was undoubtedly in religion, and in the service of religion through music" has been severely and repeatedly challenged; or, in the words of the revised edition of *The Bach Reader*, published in 1966, "whether the focus of Bach's emotional life was really 'in religion and in the service of religion through music' has been seriously questioned."[4] The basis of the challenge is in part chronological but in part also philosophical. In a historical study originally published as a long journal article in 1957 and then revised as a separate monograph in 1976, the eminent Bach scholar Alfred Dürr, known for his careful research into the manuscript tradition (as well as for extremely perceptive program notes accompanying recordings of various of the Bach cantatas), proposed, on the basis of evidence ranging from paleography to watermarks, a drastic redating of Bach's choral works composed for the church. He assigned most of the church cantatas to the years 1724/25; and, more generally, he revised the dates of composition for Bach's religious music in such a way as to remove most of it from the final twenty years of Bach's career, making 1729 the virtual *terminus ad quem* for its composition, though not of course for its performance.[5] He did admit, even in the revised edition, "the preliminary character of the results of research set down" in his monograph.[6]

Following up on Dürr's radical proposal, Friedrich Blume launched a general attack on the way Philipp Spitta, Albert Schweitzer, and others had portrayed Bach's church music, and he proposed what he called "outlines of a new picture of Bach."[7] Bach emerges from Blume's new picture as much more of a secular modern man than the conventional depictions of him had allowed, one whose attitude toward the "burden [*onus*]" of his sacred music, and even toward the organ, was profoundly ambivalent. In 1970-71 Gerhard Herz summarized, with learning and balance, the status of the controversy.[8] With acknowledgments to Herz and to Friedrich Smend (whose articles on Bach he had collected and edited as *Bach-Studien* in 1969), Christoph Wolff has sought to set the record straight and thus has provided a more balanced account. Accepting at least some of Dürr's revisionist chronology, Wolff agrees that in the 1730s Bach's "activities with the collegium [at Leipzig] must have made heavy demands on him, and the reduction in his production of sacred music is easy to understand." But he criticizes what he calls an "undue emphasis in the light of the revised dating of his works," and he rejects the conclusion "that his interest in sacred music was diminished," citing not only the *Passions*, the *Mass in B Minor*, and other later works of sacred music but also "the simple fact that, throughout his period of office, Bach provided performances of his cantatas, a repertory largely completed before 1729, every Sunday at the two main Leipzig churches," even though he may not have gone on composing new sacred works at anything even approaching the rate of his earlier productivity.[9]

The present *status controversiae* has been outlined in a recent article by John Ogasapian.[10] Ogasapian analyzes the controversy by reviewing the history of Bach interpretation, showing the strong points and the problems in both of the major alternative pictures, and presenting the reader with material to decide. In a book devoted to a review of the principal theological themes in Bach's sacred music, there has been an almost unavoidable tilting in the direction of supposing that this music represents the real Bach. In the perception of Bach by the musical public, on the other hand, the nonliturgical aspects of his creative output often predominate. Although it is estimated that about 75 percent of the more than one thousand compositions in the Schmieder catalogue (*BWV*) were composed for performance during worship services or at any rate in churches, it may well be that the remaining 25 percent are performed in concert halls and on the air 75 percent of the time—or more. Despite the highly publicized "Baroque revival," moreover, American churches, most of which stand in other traditions of hymnology and sacred music than that of Bach, have not been able to make up for that imbalance. The undeniable circumstance that most of those who listen to Bach today may find it impossible to resonate to his sacred music except as nonprogrammatic music, for which the chorales and other texts being analyzed here are at best irrelevant and at worst distracting, does not provide historians of music or historians of eighteenth-century theology with any justification for a radical secularization of Bach himself or of his sacred music.

At the same time, the revisionism of Dürr and even of Blume does serve to correct not only some of the excesses of Spitta and Schweitzer but, above all, the hagiography that depicts Bach as the unambiguously staunch orthodox Lutheran. A particularly outspoken example of such hagiography is an essay prepared for the bicentennial of Bach's death, entitled "Bach the Preacher":

We do not hear the sermons of Luther. We read them as we read the sermons of other great preachers who have long since joined the Church triumphant. We do, however, hear Bach's sermons. The works of other great musicians speak to us, but the works of Bach preach to us. These sermons, his cantatas, and particularly his *St. Matthew Passion*, proclaim the glory of the God of the Bible in a thousand voices. . . . Pastor Erdmann Neumeister of Hamburg . . . knew Bach to be a staunch Lutheran, and he knew that Bach preached God's Word in his own powerful way. When historians claim this man only as an artist of highest rank they do him an injustice.[11]

This simplistic portrait of the "staunchly Lutheran" Bach, with its polemic against historians, even went so far as to interpret 1717 to 1723, the years at Cöthen,[12] where Bach's duties were essentially secular and where there is every indication that he was as happy in his musical vocation as he ever was, as a time when "he seems to have lost sight of his goal in life. But this only lasted from 1717 to 1723. Then Bach was back in his true element again."[13] Ironically, such a one-sided resolution of the question of "sacred and secular" in Bach falls into the very Pietism and subjectivism that it uses him to oppose.

More gravely, however, it falls into a theological and musicological version of what an eminent literary theorist, William K. Wimsatt, has called "the intentional fallacy," the methodological assumption that we are to probe into what the author of a work of literature (or, in this case, the composer of a work of sacred music) "had in mind" in order to understand the work properly.[14] Wimsatt finds such probing "to belong to an art separate from criticism—to a psychological discipline, a system of self-development, a yoga . . . but . . . something different from the public art of evaluating poems" or works of music. Indeed, the very nature of music, in its function as an accompaniment to words and yet as an aesthetic entity distinct from the words, would seem to make it even less susceptible to such "intentional" interpretation than the text itself is. And that would apply above all to sacred music, especially when it arose not solely out of the composer's private and subjective "varieties of religious experience" but out of a public office and vocation as cantor, *Kapellmeister,* and church musician.

Bach's chorale preludes for the organ are a particularly fascinating case study of that methodological problem: composed to anticipate and to prepare for the congregational singing of a chorale in the setting of public worship, as the chorale was assigned to the Sunday of the church year within the "four seasons,"[15] they stand in a dynamic relation with the poetry of the hymn. Yet they could also become, both in improvisations and in prepared variations, works of artistry and virtuosity in which the text is almost, though never quite completely, out of the awareness of composer, performer, and hearer (as Bach's critics, in his own time and since, have frequently complained). Of course it may help to know what were the circumstances in the composer's life—physical and mental health, family, finances, and the like—when a particular piece of music came into being, be it a Bach cantata or Gustav Mahler's heartbreaking "Kindertotenlieder," which, Bruno Walter says, "contain perhaps the most sublime examples of the lofty heights he had reached in his orchestration."[16] But once composed and presented, the work is a public document, which must be treated as an artifact in its own right, having now a life and a reality of its own, one not functioning any longer as an extension of the composer's personality and therefore not to be interpreted primarily as an extension of the composer's biography.

The pietistic or romantic subjectivism that professes to be able to discern Bach's Lutheran orthodoxy in his "sacred" music as such must inevitably founder on his "secular" music, for any supposed musical difference between Bach's sacred music and his secular music cannot establish itself as empirically demonstrable. A fine illustration is the so-called "Air for the G String." Its very beauty as a melody has caused it to suffer from the ingenuity of adapters and orchestrators, as well as of conductors, so that performances of it sometimes sound more like Johannes Brahms or even Richard Wagner than like Johann Sebastian Bach. As Denis Arnold has commented,

> The grand French-style overture in D major for full orchestra, in which the dance material included the famous air, arranged quite unnecessarily by Wilhelmj for playing on the G string, [was] in its original version simply a very beautiful decorative aria in Bach's customary style, the phrases spun out delicately to form that seamless melody which confounded singers by its lack of breathing pauses, but goes well on violins.[17]

But it has demonstrated its durability and vitality by surviving such treatment to be and remain one of Bach's most memorable melodic achievements. And, like the Tchaikovsky "Andante cantabile," to which it has often been compared, the "Air for the G String" evokes in many of its listeners a response that can only be characterized as "devotional," even though it belongs to Bach's "secular" works. Does it become more authentically "devotional" when someone adds a set of religious words to it? Conversely, the duet "Wir eilen mit schwachen, doch emsigen Schritten [We hasten with timid but diligent paces]," from the cantata (*BWV* 78) "Jesu, der du meine Seele [Jesus, thou who this my spirit]" (Ambrose, *Cantatas* 200–203), has recently been transcribed for brass quintet. More familiarly, the aria "Liebster Jesu, mein Verlangen [Dearest Jesus, my desiring]," which opens the cantata (*BWV* 32) of that name (Ambrose, *Cantatas* (97–99), has likewise gone through several instrumental transformations, from full modern orchestra to synthesizer to flute, in which the original words have long since disappeared. Are these two, the duet and the aria, no longer authentically "devotional" because they have been shorn of their texts as parts of Bach's "sacred cantatas"?

This reference to "sacred cantatas" may serve as a reminder that not all of Bach's cantatas were "sacred." He seems to have composed many cantatas—at any rate, many more than have been preserved—for various altogether secular occasions. By Wolff's counting, "about two-fifths of Bach's sacred cantatas must be considered lost," while "of the secular cantatas, more are lost than survive."[18] As Spitta notes, "At that time people chose the street, the garden, the wood, or even the lake or river, according to whether the music to be performed referred to a public ceremony, a wedding, a birthday, a hunting expedition, or any other festivity."[19] One of the most familiar of the "secular cantatas" of Bach is the so-called Peasant Cantata (*BWV* 212), "Mer hahn en neue Oberkeet [We have a new administration]," composed on a text in German dialect by Picander for the inauguration of Carl Heinrich von Dieskau as the new lord of the Kleinzschocher estate near Leipzig on 30 August 1742. Christoph Wolff, noting that "this work is unique in Bach's output for its folklike manner," observes:

> The thoroughly up-to-date characteristics of parts of the work show that Bach was not only intimately acquainted with the musical fashions of the times but also knew how to adapt elements of the

younger generation's style for his own purposes. . . . This work [was] apparently his last secular cantata.[20]

A hearer who is best acquainted with the church cantatas experiences, in listening to the Peasant Cantata, considerable amusement at finding many of the familiar techniques adapted here to a rollicking folk festival, which could have been illustrated with a painting by Pieter Brueghel the Elder.[21] Perhaps there are also some hearers who sense occasional vexation at the ease with which Bach has been able to move back and forth between the genre of the "sacred cantata" and the genre of the "secular cantata."

If any hearers, pious or not, do experience such vexation over the "secular cantatas," the "amazement" will be vastly increased if they go on to a study of Bach's compositional practice, even though, as Arnold Schering says, "it is understandable in both human and artistic terms."[22] The *Christmas Oratorio* (*BWV* 248) is especially notable for its use of Luther's "Christmas carol for children" (*Ein Kinderlied auf die Weihnacht*), "Vom Himmel hoch da komm' ich her,"[23] and for its transposition, in the very last chorus of part 6, of what is usually regarded as a Lenten chorale into a paean of Christmas victory.[24] But a substantial percentage of the music in parts 1 through 5 of the *Christmas Oratorio* was in fact recycled from three secular cantatas (*BWV* 213–15), composed by Bach during the autumns of 1733 and 1734. On 3 September 1733, on the occasion of the birthday of Prince Friedrich Christian, Bach had presented *BWV* 213, "Hercules auf dem Scheidewege: Lasst uns sorgen, lasst uns wachen [Hercules at the crossroads]"; on 8 December 1733, for the birthday of the Electress Maria Josepha, he prepared *BWV* 214, "Tönet, ihr Pauken! Erschallet, Trompeten! [Resound, you kettledrums! Sound, you trumpets!]"; and for the anniversary of the election of Elector Augustus III as king of Poland,[25] 5 October 1734, he wrote the patriotic cantata, *BWV* 215, "Preise dein Glück, gesegnetes Sachsen [Praise your good fortune, blessed Saxony]."

Yet he had no compunctions about taking these three works, which are secular in content and all but operatic in style, setting Christmas words to them for (presumably) many of the same people who had heard the secular works, adding a substantial amount of other and new material, and putting it all on during the six feast days of Christmas of 1734/35, from Christmas Day to Epiphany, as the oratorio *Die heilige Weihnacht,* for performance in church. Perhaps even more striking is the comparison between the works listed in the Schmieder catalogue as *BWV* 249 and *BWV* 249a. The first of these in the numbering, *BWV* 249, is the *Easter Oratorio,* whose final version dates from 1732/35. But *BWV* 249a, though second in the numbering, is the secular cantata "Entfliehet, ver-schwindet, entweichet, ihr Sorgen! [You worries, run away, disap-pear, yield!]," which he had originally prepared for the birthday of Duke Christian of Saxe-Weissenfels on 23 February 1725. Indeed, he had taken that secular cantata of February 1725 and presented it on 1 April of the same year as an Easter cantata, before revising it several years later into the oratorio. What is more, the text of the secular cantata and the text of the oratorio both came from the same librettist, Christian Friedrich Heinrici, usually called Picander.

What happens to the distinction between the "sacred" and the "secular" Bach in the light of his concrete practice as a composer? Clearly Bach's compositional thrift compelled him not to waste any-thing but to use words and especially melodies over again when they seemed to fit: after composing a melody for Picander's text, "Es lebe der König! [Long live the king!]" (*BWV* Anhang 11), he turned it into the "Osanna in excelsis" of the *Mass in B Minor.* But it was not merely the circumstances of his employment that led to this compositional practice. Much less can he be said to "have lost sight of his goal" when, as in Cöthen, he composed "secular" music. Rather, if, as that very *Mass in B Minor* suggests,[26] it was the privilege of the composer's spirit to praise God in writing the "Osanna in excelsis," he could do so also when he was not compos-ing for the church, as he did in writing "Es lebe der König!"—and both on the same melody.

Bach's craftsmanship as an organ builder corroborates this under-standing of "sacred" and "secular" in his lifework. Already in the early years of his career he was deeply involved in this craft. He served as organist at Mühlhausen for scarcely one year, from June 1707 to June 1708; and "it is," as Arnold puts it, "at Mühlhausen that Bach the composer appears."[27] But it was also there that Bach the designer and engineer showed his powers. Bach's memorandum of 21 February 1708, containing his detailed plans, pipe by pipe, for the reconstruction of the organ at the Church of Saint Blaise (Divus Blasius) in Mühlhausen, has been preserved.[28] It is clear from Bach's comments on the manuscript of Jacob Adlung's *Musica Mechanica Organoedi* (which was not published until after both the author and Bach had died), as well as from other contemporary biographical information, how methodically Bach went about the task of evaluating an existing instrument and making recommendations for its improvement. Johann Nikolaus Forkel has drawn a charming portrait:

> He was very severe, but always just, in his trials of organs. As he was perfectly acquainted with the construction of the instrument, he could not be in any case deceived. The first thing he did in trying out an organ was to draw out all the stops and to play with the full organ. He used to say in jest that he must first of all know whether the instrument had good lungs. He then proceeded to examine the single parts.[29]

The attitude reflected in this craftsmanship bespeaks the conviction of Luther and the Reformers that the performance of any God-pleasing vocation was the service of God, even if it did not lead to the performance of chorales. The Bach of the Peasant Cantata, the partitas, and the concertos was not "too secular." These were, rather, the expression of a unitary (if to modern eyes sometimes inconsistent or even self-contradictory) world view, in which all beauty, including "secular" beauty, was sacred because God was one, both Creator and Redeemer.

Thus observation of the craftsmanship evident in Bach's use of cello and violone, now often replaced by the contrabass, in his suites and other "secular" works is an indispensable preparation for the understanding of the role of these instruments in his "sacred" works. That use of the cello becomes evident, for example, in the aria "Et exaltavit spiritus meus [And my spirit hath rejoiced]" from the *Magnificat* (*BWV* 243), and repeatedly in the *Passion according to Saint John*, where the cello is at least as important as the harpsichord in providing the continuo and also (for example, in the alto aria "Es ist vollbracht"[30]) in carrying on a dialogue with the parts for solo voices. Perhaps because several of its sections had been recycled from earlier "secular" works,[31] the *B Minor Mass* is rich in such use of cello and especially of contrabass: in the opening "Kyrie," in the bass quarter notes throughout the opening chorus of the "Credo," in the cello and bass accompaniment for the "Confiteor" and the "Osanna in excelsis," in the solemn basses during the "Sanctus." Surely it would be impossible to argue that such craftsmanship was essentially different when Bach adapted it to the purposes of the *Mass* from what it had been in the earlier versions of the same music, or from what it is in the *Musical Offering*. Spitta may think that in the cantata (*BWV* 176) "Es ist ein trotzig und verzagt Ding [There is a daring and a shy thing about the human spirit]" (Ambrose, *Cantatas* 414–16), the first aria, "in the style of a gavotte," is "charming as a piece of music, but quite unsuited to its text."[32] But this "gavotte" was the expression of a spirit that had dedicated even its humor to the adoration of the Holy.

Like most other towering figures in our tradition, Johann Sebastian Bach seems to have been a "complex of opposites," and the new picture of him that is emerging from recent research only accentuates this quality in him and in his work. He especially resembles Martin Luther, whose collected works he owned and from whom he quoted not only chorales but riddles,[33] in combining a simplicity, almost a naiveté, at one level, with not only profundity but ambiguity at another. Bach the man continues to puzzle his biographers, friendly or unfriendly, and by all indications he will go on doing so. Perhaps it would be appropriate to conclude by giving one of the most recent of his biographers almost the last word about the task of understanding him:

> Bach may have been a mystic, an ecstatic—but that view may shed more light on Schweitzer's mentality than his subject's. He may have been a convinced Lutheran who sought his salvation in writing music and persuading others to virtue. He may be considered the last of the medieval craftsmen in music, the product of a Germany which missed the Renaissance. All this is speculation. What is not is that he was a thoroughly professional musician, doing his job day in, day out.[34]

This is *almost* the last word, because even this new (and yet very old) sacred-*cum*-secular Johann Sebastian Bach began his compositions by writing "*Jesu Juva* [Jesus, help]" and closed them by writing "*Soli Deo Gloria* [to God alone be the glory]."

Notes

1. THE FOUR SEASONS
OF J. S. BACH

1. David-Mendel, *Bach Reader,* 28.

2. Wolff, *Bach Family,* 122.

3. Hans-Günter Klein, *Der Einfluss der vivaldischen Konzertform im Instrumentalwerk Johann Sebastian Bachs* (Strasbourg, 1970).

4. Anne Thorn Higgins, "Time and the English Corpus Christi Drama" (Ph.D. diss., Yale University, 1985), 22.

5. See, e.g., Jaroslav Pelikan, "The Two Sees of Peter," in *The Shaping of Christianity in the Second and Third Centuries,* ed. E. P. Sanders (Philadelphia: Fortress Press, 1980), 57–73.

6. Louis Duchesne, "La question de la Pâque au concile de Nicée," *Revue des questions historiques* 28 (1880): 1–42.

7. Charles W. Jones, Introduction, in Bede, *Opera de Temporibus,* ed. Charles W. Jones (Cambridge, Mass.: Mediaeval Academy of America, 1943), 3–122.

8. Oscar Cullmann, "The Origins of Christmas," in *The Early Church: Studies in Early Christian History and Theology,* ed. A. J. B. Higgins (Philadelphia: Westminster Press, 1956), 17–36.

9. Peter Browe, "Zur Geschichte des Dreifaltigkeitsfestes," *Archiv für Liturgiewissenschaft* 1 (1950): 65–81.

10. David-Mendel, *Bach Reader,* 65–66.

11. Erdmann Neumeister, *Christlicher Unterricht wie die h. Adventszeit, das h. Christ-Fest und das Neue Jahr gotgefällig zu feiren sey,* 2d ed. (n.p. [Hamburg?], 1737), 1–2.

12. Ibid., 6.

13. Ibid., 7.

14. Wolff, *Bach Family,* 87–88.

15. *LBW* 312; cf. Julian, *Dictionary* 2:972–73.

16. Neumeister, *Advent*, 64.

17. Ibid., 96.

18. Ibid., 94–95.

19. Georg Kretschmar, "Himmelfahrt und Pfingsten," *Zeitschrift für Kirchengeschichte* 66 (1954): 209–53.

20. See the references in Geoffrey W. H. Lampe, ed., *A Patristic Greek Lexicon* (London: Oxford University Press, 1961), 1060, s.v.

21. Eusebius, *Life of Constantine* 4.64 (*NPNF* 1:557).

22. For detailed references, see Jaroslav Pelikan, *The Christian Tradition: A History of the Development of Doctrine*, 4 vols. to date (Chicago: University of Chicago Press, 1971–), 1:173, 198–200, 106–7; 4:329–30.

23. Macedonius (?), as quoted by Gregory of Nazianzus, *Theological Orations* 5.12 (*NPNF* 7:321).

24. Jaroslav Pelikan, "The 'Spiritual Sense' of Scripture: The Exegetical Basis for Saint Basil's Doctrine of the Holy Spirit," in *Basil of Caesarea: Christian, Humanist, Ascetic*, ed. Paul Jonathan Fedwick, 2 vols. (Toronto: Pontifical Institute of Mediaeval Studies, 1981), 1:337–60.

25. Julian, *Dictionary* 2:1206–11.

26. Ibid., 1:821; 1:631–32.

27. Martin Luther, *Against the Heavenly Prophets*, LW 40:83; *On the Councils and the Church*, LW 41:114.

28. Regin Prenter, *Spiritus Creator*, trans. John M. Jensen (Philadelphia: Muhlenberg Press, 1953), is probably the most important scholarly effort to redress the balance in the study of Luther's doctrine of the Holy Spirit.

29. Schweitzer, *Bach* 1:292; 2:69.

30. Smend, *Bach-Studien*, 195–211, "Bachs Himmelfahrts-Oratorium."

31. Spitta, *Bach* 3:47.

32. Ibid., 2:367.

33. Wolff, *Bach Family*, 84.

34. Ralph Kirkpatrick, *Interpreting Bach's "Well-Tempered Clavier"* (New Haven: Yale University Press, 1984), 31.

35. Spitta, *Bach* 3:107.

36. See especially chap. 6, below.

37. See chap. 8, below.

38. Schweitzer, *Bach* 1:411, note.

39. Spitta, *Bach* 1:456–64.

40. Schweitzer, *Bach* 2:125–26.

2. THE MUSICAL HERITAGE
OF THE REFORMATION

1. Valentin Ernst Loescher, *Drey Predigten von der Erkänntniss und Ehre des Sohnes Gottes* (Dresden and Neustadt, 1733), 28–30. On the "Evangelical Salzburgers," see the article of that title in *PRE* 17:408–15.

2. *PRE* 2:465.

3. Sigmund Jakob Baumgarten, *Predigten,* 3 vols. (Halle, 1756–59), 1:385–440.

4. See the memoir of Eduard Devrient, "Mendelssohn's Revival of the St. Matthew Passion," in David-Mendel, *Bach Reader,* 376–86.

5. Bernhard Friedrich Richter, "Über die Schicksale der Thomasschule zu Leipzig angehörenden Kantaten Joh. Seb. Bachs," *BJb* 3 (1906): 61.

6. Schweitzer, *Bach* 2:90–91, with musical examples.

7. Spitta, *Bach* 2:470–71.

8. Wilhelm Dilthey, *Weltanschauung und Analyse des Menschen seit Renaissance und Reformation* (Stuttgart, 1964), 515.

9. Kurt Aland, *Hilfsbuch zum Lutherstudium* (Gütersloh, n.d.), no. 415.

10. Théodore Gérold, "Protestant Music on the Continent," in *The Age of Humanism 1540–1630,* ed. Gerald Abraham, vol. 4 of *New Oxford History of Music* (London: Oxford University Press, 1968), 419, 422.

11. Neumeister, *Räuch-Opfer,* 493–94.

12. *TLH* 266.

13. See chap. 1, above.

14. *BWV* 245, no. 9.

15. Einar Billing, *Our Calling,* trans. Conrad Bergendoff (Rock Island, Ill.: Augustana, 1952), 7.

16. See Julian, *Dictionary* 1:96–97, also on various English translations.

17. See chap. 6, below.

18. Schweitzer, *Bach* 2:70–71.

19. Rudolf Hermann, *Luthers These "Gerecht und Sunder zugleich"* (Gütersloh, 1960), 1.

20. Here as elsewhere, I am indebted to the pioneering research of Gerhard Ebeling, *Evangelische Evangelienauslegung* (Munich, 1942).

21. Smend, *Bach-Studien,* 90–109, "Bachs Kanonwerk über 'Vom Himmel hoch da komm' ich her.' "

22. Igor Stravinsky and Robert Craft, *Conversations with Igor Stravinsky* (Berkeley and Los Angeles: University of California Press, 1980), 31.

23. Paul Henry Lang, ed., *Stravinsky: A New Appraisal of His Work* (New York: W. W. Norton & Co., 1963), 116.

24. Quoted in Roman Vlad, *Stravinsky,* trans. Frederick and Ann Fuller (London: Oxford University Press, 1960), 197.

25. Smend, *Bach-Studien,* 163, "Luther und Bach."

26. I have, in what follows, adapted some of the material in my *Obedient Rebels: Catholic Substance and Protestant Principle in Luther's Reformation* (New York: Harper & Row, 1964), 77–104.

27. *LW* 53:15–40; 51–90.

28. Paul Hindemith, *Johann Sebastian Bach: Heritage and Obligation* (New Haven: Yale University Press, 1952), 28–29.

29. Ibid., 42.

3. RATIONALISM AND *AUFKLÄRUNG* IN BACH'S CAREER

1. James Collins, Preface, in Rosemary Z. Lauer, *The Mind of Voltaire: A Study in His Constructive Deism* (Westminster, Md.: Newman Press, 1961), ix.

2. Peter Gay, *The Enlightenment: An Interpretation*, 2 vols. (New York: Alfred A. Knopf, 1966–69), 2:243–44.

3. Ibid., 2:243.

4. Wolff, *Bach Family*, 108.

5. David-Mendel, *Bach Reader*, 23.

6. Ibid., 176.

7. Christoph Wolff, "Überlegungen zum 'Thema Regium,'" *BJb* 60 (1974):37.

8. Christoph Wolff, "New Research on Bach's Musical Offering," *Musical Quarterly* 57 (1971):379.

9. Wolff, *Bach Family*, 162.

10. Johannes Rüber, *Bach and the Heavenly Choir*, trans. Maurice Michael (Cleveland and New York: World Publishing Co., 1956), 128–30.

11. Harry Austryn Wolfson, *The Philosophy of Spinoza: Unfolding the Latent Processes of His Reasoning*, 2 vols. (Cambridge, Mass.: Harvard University Press, 1962), 1:53.

12. Martin C. D'Arcy, "The Philosophy of St. Augustine," in *Saint Augustine*, Martin C. D'Arcy and others (New York: Meridian Books, 1957), 169.

13. Ernst Cassirer, *The Philosophy of the Enlightenment*, trans. Fritz C. A. Koelln and James P. Pettegrove (Princeton: Princeton University Press, 1951), 15.

14. Thomas Aquinas, *Summa Theologica*, Part I, question 1, article 2.

15. *Confessions* 10. 33. 49, in Albert C. Outler, ed. and trans., *Augustine: Confessions and Enchiridion*, Library of Christian Classics, vol. 7 (Philadelphia: Westminster Press, 1955), p. 230.

16. John Dryden, "A Song for St. Cecilia's Day," *The Oxford Book of English Verse 1250–1918* (London: Oxford University Press, 1955), 479.

17. Dryden, "Alexander's Feast or The Power of Music. An Ode in Honour of St. Cecilia's Day, 1967 [*sic*]," *The New Oxford Book of English Verse 1250–1950* (London: Oxford University Press, 1972), 383.

18. Wilhelm Werker, *Studien über die Symmetrie im Bau der Fugen und die motivische Zusammengehörigkeit der Präludien und Fugen des "Wohltemperierten Klaviers" von J. S. Bach* (Leipzig, 1922), 331.

19. Martin Jansen, "Bachs Zahlensymbolik, an seinen Passionen untersucht," *BJb*, 34 (1937): 104.

20. Urlich Siegele, *Bachs theologischer Formbegriff und das Duett F-Dur* (Neuhausen and Stuttgart, 1978), 21–26.

21. David-Mendel, *Bach Reader*, 224.

22. Ibid., 32.

23. Ibid., 155.

24. Gay, *Enlightenment* 2:219.

25. Ibid., 517.

26. Henry F. May, *The Enlightenment in America* (New York: Oxford University Press, 1976), 216–17.

27. Martin Petzoldt, "Zwischen Orthodoxie, Pietismus und Aufklärung: Überlegungen zum theologiegeschichtlichen Kontext Johann Sebastian Bachs," Szeskus, *Aufklärung,* 66–108.

28. John Stroup, *The Struggle for Identity in the Clerical Estate* (Leiden, 1984), 82–85.

29. Johann Heinrich Campe, quoted in Stroup, *Struggle for Clerical Identity,* 116.

30. C. F. George Heinrici, "Ernesti, Johann August," *PRE* 5:469–74.

31. Johann Wolfgang von Goethe, *The Autobiography of Johann Wolfgang von Goethe,* trans. John Oxenford, introd. Karl J. Weintraub, 2 vols. (Chicago: University of Chicago Press, 1975), 1:258, 275.

32. Paul S. Minear, "J. S. Bach and J. A. Ernesti: A Case Study in Exegetical and Theological Conflict," in John Deschner and others, eds., *Our Common History as Christians: Essays in Honor of Albert C. Outler* (New York: Oxford University Press, 1975), 131–55.

33. David-Mendel, *Bach Reader,* 158; the documents themselves appear on 137–49, 152–58.

34. Ibid., 155, 145.

35. Spitta, *Bach* 3:13; Schweitzer, *Bach* 1:143.

36. J. F. Kohler, *Historia Scholarum Lipsiensium,* in David-Mendel, *Bach Reader,* 137.

37. Spitta, *Bach* 3:15.

38. Emanuel Hirsch, *Geschichte der neuern evangelischen Theologie,* 5 vols. (Gütersloh, 1960), 4:11.

39. Minear, "Bach and Ernesti," 137.

40. See chap. 10, below.

41. See the brief discussion in Julian, *Dictionary* 1:319.

42. Schweitzer, *Bach* 1:223–24.

43. André Pirro, *J. S. Bach,* trans. Mervyn Savill (New York: Crown Publishers, 1957), 59–60.

44. Quoted in Spitta, *Bach* 3:275.

4. CONFESSIONAL ORTHODOXY
IN BACH'S RELIGION

1. Erdmann Neumeister, *De poetis germanicis,* ed. Franz Heiduk (Bern, 1978).

2. David-Mendel, *Bach Reader,* 80.

3. Reprinted in David-Mendel, *Bach Reader,* 81–82.

4. "Vorrede," in Erdmann Neumeister, *Psalmen und Lobgesänge und geistliche Lieder* (n.p., n.d. [Hamburg?, 1755?]), 4Av.

5. Quoted by Spitta, *Bach* 1:474, whose entire discussion of Neumeister, pp. 470–82, puts him into the context of the eighteenth century.

6. Hermann Beck, "Neumeister, Erdmann," in *PRE* 13:772.

7. Neumeister, *Räuch-Opfer,* Preface, A3r.

8. Ibid., 90–91, 176.

9. See the discussion in Julian, *Dictionary* 1:352–53.

10. Neumeister, *Räuch-Opfer,* 495.

11. Ambrose's translation, in faithfulness to the original, also reverts to "murd'rous Pope and Turk."

12. Abraham Calovius, *Die Heilige Bibel,* 3 vols. (Wittenberg, 1681), in the library of Concordia Seminary, Saint Louis, Missouri.

13. Acts 4:12; Augustine, *On the Trinity* 15.25.44.

14. Calov, *Bibel* 1:504.

15. Neumeister, *Räuch-Opfer,* 782–83.

16. Neumeister, *Advent,* 65–80.

17. See chap. 2, above.

18. Schweitzer, *Bach* 2:318–19.

19. See chap. 1, above.

20. For a careful analysis, see Jost Casper, "Die Auslegungstradition der Kantata BWV 140," Petzoldt, *Ausleger* 49–76.

21. Pelikan, *Christian Tradition* 1:173.

22. David-Mendel, *Bach Reader,* 65.

23. Smalcald Articles 2.4.10, *The Book of Concord,* ed. Theodore G. Tappert and others (Philadelphia: Muhlenberg Press, 1959), 300.

24. On the successive versions of this motto, see *The Oxford Dictionary of Quotations,* 3d ed. (New York: Oxford University Press, 1980), 338.

25. Neumeister, *Räuch-Opfer,* A3v.

26. Ibid., 535.

27. See the detailed article, based in part on unprinted sources, by Paul Tschakert, *PRE* 18:625–31.

28. See the brief description by Spitta, *Bach* 2:461.

29. Schweitzer, *Bach* 2:83.

30. Ibid., 373.

31. Neumeister, *Advent,* 4–5.

32. Wolff, *Bach Family,* 65, 126.

33. Ibid., 80, 86.

34. See chap. 10, below.

5. PIETISM, PIETY, AND DEVOTION
IN BACH'S CANTATAS

1. Carl Mirbt, "Pietismus," *PRE* 15:782–83.

2. See the detailed presentation on "Moravian Hymnody" in Julian, *Dictionary* 1:765–69.

3. Neumeister, *Räuch-Opfer*, 58.

4. Spitta, *Bach* 1:164–70.

5. Julian, *Dictionary* 1:311; 2:1038.

6. Petzoldt, *Ausleger*, 12.

7. Peter C. Erb, ed., *The Pietists: Selected Writings*, Classics of Western Spirituality (New York: Paulist Press, 1983), xiii.

8. *The Oxford Dictionary of the Christian Church*, rev. ed. (New York: Oxford University Press, 1983), 805.

9. Philipp Jakob Spener, *Pia Desideria*, ed. and trans. Theodore G. Tappert (Philadelphia: Fortress Press, 1964).

10. Ibid., 107.

11. Ibid., 95.

12. Spitta, *Bach* 3:109–12.

13. Arnold Schering, "Bach und das Schemellische Gesangbuch," *BJb* 21 (1924):123.

14. See chap. 6, below.

15. Joseph Sittler, "Johann Sebastian Bach: An Essay in Discovery," *The Cresset*, April 1943, 16–23.

16. Pelikan, *Christian Tradition* 1:278–331.

17. See chap. 2, above.

18. August Hermann Francke, "Rules for the Protection of Conscience and for Good Order in Conversation or in Society," in Erb, *Pietists*, 111.

19. Probably the best known of these was Tertullian's *De spectaculis*, *ANF* 3:79–91.

20. C. F. W. Walther, *Tanz und Theaterbesuch* (Saint Louis, 1885).

21. See my introduction, "Walther's *Law and Gospel* in Historical Perspective," in the centennial edition of Carl F. Walther, *The Proper Distinction Between the Law and the Gospel*, trans. W. H. T. Dau (Saint Louis, Mo.: Concordia Publishing House, 1985).

22. Walther, *Law and Gospel*, 362–63.

23. Z. Philip Ambrose, " 'Weinen, Klagen, Sorgen, Zagen' und die antike Redekunst," *BJb* 66 (1980): 35–45.

24. See chap. 10, below.

25. Johann Albrecht Bengel, *Abriss der so genannten Brüdergemeinde* (Stuttgart, 1751), 125.

26. See chap. 7, below.

27. Kerala Johnson Snyder, "Buxtehude, Dietrich," *New Grove* 3:535.

28. Johann Wilhelm Petersen, *Die Hochzeit des Lammes und der Braut* (Offenbach am Main, 1701), 198–99.

29. See chap. 4, above.

30. Julian, *Dictionary* 2:1014.

31. Schweitzer, *Bach* 1:12.

32. *Cambridge Modern History* 4:418.

33. On the whole subject, see James Midgley Clark, *The Dance of Death in the Middle Ages and the Renaissance* (Glasgow: Jackson, Son & Co., 1950).

34. *Saint John Passion*, no. 32.

35. Pirro, *Bach*, 112.

36. Schweitzer, *Bach* 2:77.

37. See chap. 6, below.

6. THEMES AND VARIATIONS IN
THE BACH *PASSIONS*

1. Alfred Einstein, *Mozart: His Character, His Work*, trans. Arthur Mendel and Nathan Broder (New York: Oxford University Press, 1945), 119.

2. Walter James Turner, *Mozart: The Man and His Works* (1938; Garden City, N.Y.: Doubleday & Co., 1954), 271.

3. Martin Geck, *Die Wiederentdeckung der Matthäuspassion im 19. Jahrhundert* (Regensburg, 1967), especially 34–60.

4. Bach, *Saint Matthew Passion*, no. 74 (Gen. 3:8; 8:11).

5. Winton Dean and Anthony Hicks, "Handel, George Frideric," *New Grove* 8:83–140.

6. Julian, *Dictionary* 2:1287.

7. Reprinted in George Bernard Shaw, *The Great Composers: Reviews and Bombardments*, ed. Louis Crompton (Berkeley and Los Angeles: University of California Press, 1978), 238–42.

8. Spitta, *Bach* 2:544.

9. See chap. 7, below.

10. Johann Friedrich Mayer, *Geistliche Reden* (Berlin, 1702), 745–46.

11. Bach, *Saint Matthew Passion*, no. 3; *Saint John Passion*, no. 7.

12. Bach, *Saint Matthew Passion*, nos. 25, 55.

13. Bach, *Saint John Passion*, no. 27; see also chap. 8, below.

14. Schweitzer, *Bach* 2:69–70.

15. See chap. 8, below.

16. Spitta, *Bach* 2:553.

17. L. Hoffmann-Erbrecht, "Haszler, Hans Leo," in *LTK* 5:26.

18. See chap. 5, above.

19. Julian, *Dictionary* 1:125–26.

20. Walter Blankenburg, "Hassler, Hans Leo," *New Grove* 8:296.

21. *The Penguin Book of Latin Verse*, ed. Frederick Brittain (Baltimore: Penguin Books, 1962), 236–39.

22. Julian, *Dictionary* 1:835.

23. Bach, *Saint Matthew Passion*, nos. 17, 20.

24. Ibid., no. 21.

25. Ibid., no. 23.

26. Ibid., nos. 17, 22.

27. Helmut Rilling, *Johann Sebastian Bach: St. Matthew Passion*, trans. Kenneth Nafziger (Frankfurt, 1976), 35.

28. Bach, *Saint Matthew Passion,* nos. 52–53.
29. Ibid., no. 63.
30. Ibid., no. 72.
31. See chap. 8, below.

7. "MEDITATION ON HUMAN REDEMPTION" IN THE *SAINT MATTHEW PASSION*

1. Charles H. Talbert, Introduction, in Hermann Samuel Reimarus, *Fragments,* ed. Charles H. Talbert; trans. Ralph S. Fraser (Philadelphia: Fortress Press, 1970), 6.
2. Reimarus, *Fragments,* 149–50; italics added.
3. Bach, *Saint Matthew Passion,* no. 71.
4. Ibid., nos. 54, 59.
5. Ibid., nos. 57–58.
6. Vincent of Lérins, *Commonitory,* chap. 2 (*NPNF* 11:132).
7. Luther, Smalcald Articles 2.2.11, *Book of Concord,* ed. Theodore G. Tappert and others, 294.
8. John Calvin, *Institutes of the Christian Religion,* ed. John T. McNeill, 2 vols., Library of Christian Classics, vols. 20, 21 (Philadelphia: Westminster Press, 1960), 4.18.12–18 (2:1440–46).
9. Pelikan, *Christian Tradition* 1:146–47, 168–69.
10. Ibid., 3:79–80, 136–37, 188–90.
11. Anselm, *Why God Became Man,* Preface, *Anselm of Canterbury,* 4 vols., (Lewiston, N.Y.: Edwin Mellen Press, 1974), trans. Jasper Hopkins and Herbert Richardson, 3:6.
12. Hopkins and Richardson, 1:137–44.
13. See chap. 9, below.
14. Pelikan, *Christian Tradition* 4:161–62, 238, 282.
15. Neumeister, *Festgegründeter Beweis . . . dasz Jesus Christus für uns und unsere Sünden gnung gthan,* 2d ed. ([Hamburg], 1730), A6v-A7r.
16. Neumeister, *Beweis,* 50.
17. Neumeister, *Räuch-Opfer,* 56.
18. Neumeister, *Beweis,* 104–5.
19. Ibid., 148.
20. Pelikan, *Christian Tradition* 4:359–61.
21. It will be evident that I am indebted to, among others, Smend, *Bach-Studien,* 24–83: "Bachs Matthäus-Passion: Untersuchungen zur Geschichte des Werkes bis 1750."
22. Rilling, *St. Matthew Passion,* 14.
23. Julian, *Dictionary* 1:517, s.v. "Herzliebster Jesu."
24. Bach, *Saint Matthew Passion,* no. 25.
25. Ibid., no. 31.
26. Ibid., no. 71.

27. See chap. 6, above.
28. Bach, *Saint Matthew Passion*, no. 35.
29. Ibid., no. 47.
30. Ibid., no. 50.
31. Ibid., no. 51.
32. Apology 12.8, *Book of Concord*, 183.
33. Bach, *Saint Matthew Passion*, nos. 56, 59.
34. Ibid., no. 69.
35. See chap. 6, above.
36. Bach, *Saint Matthew Passion*, no. 72.
37. Ibid., no. 77.
38. Ibid., no. 76.

8. "CHRISTUS VICTOR" IN THE
SAINT JOHN PASSION

1. See chap. 2, above.
2. Ernst König, "Neuerkenntnisse zu J. S. Bachs Köthener Zeit," *BJb* 57 (1957): 163–67.
3. See chap. 10, below.
4. Schweitzer, *Bach* 1:107.
5. Many of Werenfels's occasional works are collected in his *Opuscula theologica, philosophica, et philologica*, 3d ed., 2 vols. (Lyon, 1772).
6. See Eberhard Vischer, "Werenfels, Samuel," *PRE* 21:106–10.
7. Werenfels, *Opuscula* 1:323–42.
8. Ibid., 343–74.
9. Ibid., 481–83.
10. "Dissertatio in verba Domini: 'Hoc est corpus meum,' " Werenfels, *Opuscula* 1:179.
11. Augustine, *On the Psalms* 130.3.5 (*NPNF* 8:613–14).
12. Pelikan, *Christian Tradition* 4:359–61.
13. John Calvin, *Institutes of the Christian Religion* 4.18.3, McNeill ed., 2:1432.
14. Ibid., 4.18.13, McNeill ed., 2:1442.
15. On voice and instrument in this aria, see Harry Goldschmidt, "Johannes-Passion: 'Es ist vollbracht'—Zu Bachs obligatem Begleitverfahren," *Bericht über die Wissenschaftliche Konferenze zum III. Internationalen Bach-Fest der DDR*, ed. Werner Felix (Leipzig, 1977), 181–88.
16. Marshall, *Process*, 71.
17. *Saint John Passion*, no. 58.
18. Paul Steinitz, *Bach's Passions* (New York: Charles Scribner's Sons, 1979), 61.
19. Walter Serauky, "Die 'Johannes-Passion' von Joh. Seb. Bach und ihr Vorbild," *BJb* 41 (1954):29–39.

20. The standard treatment of this theory is that of Gustaf Aulén, *Christus Victor*, introd. Jaroslav Pelikan (New York: Macmillan Co., 1969).

21. Gregory of Nyssa, *The Great Catechism* 24 (*NPNF* 5:494).

22. Pelikan, *Christian Tradition* 4:160–65.

23. See the important discussion in Luther's *Galatians*, *LW* 26:276–91.

24. Pelikan, *Christian Tradition* 1:149–51; 2:138–39.

25. See chap. 3, above.

26. H. C. Erik Midelfort, *Witch Hunting in Southwestern Germany 1562–1684: The Social and Intellectual Foundations* (Stanford, Calif.: Stanford University Press, 1972), 125, quoting Hugh Trevor-Roper.

27. Basil Willey, *The Seventeenth Century Background: Studies in the Thought of the Age in Relation to Poetry and Religion* (Garden City, N.Y.: Doubleday & Co., 1953), 195–203.

28. Bach, *Saint John Passion*, no. 7.

29. Ibid., no. 9.

30. Ibid., no. 11.

31. Ibid., no. 60.

32. See chap. 6, above.

33. Bach, *Passio secundum Joannem*, no. 1, reprinted in *Boston Early Music Festival and Exhibition* (3–9 June 1985), 98–109.

34. Bach, *Passio secundum Joannem*, no. 40.

35. Smend, *Bach-Studien*, 18–19: "Die Johannes-Passion von Bach."

36. See chap. 5, above.

37. Bach, *Saint John Passion*, nos. 31–32.

38. See Schweitzer, *Bach* 1:213.

39. Bach, *Saint John Passion*, no. 19.

40. Ibid., no. 62.

41. Ibid., nos. 67, 40.

42. Ibid., nos. 60, 67.

43. See the quotation from Bengel, chap. 5, above.

44. Ferdinand Hahn, *Christologische Hoheitstitel: Ihre Geschichte im frühen Christentum* (Göttingen, 1963).

45. Gerd Rienäcker, "Beobachtungen zum Text-Musik Verhältnis im Eingangschor der Johannes-Passion von J. S. Bach," in Szeskus, *Aufklärung*, 181–82.

46. Charles Sanford Terry, *Bach: The Passions*, 2 vols. (London: Oxford University Press, 1929), 1:22.

47. Bach, *Saint John Passion*, no. 27.

48. Ibid., nos. 46, 49.

49. Ibid., no. 40.

50. Ibid., no. 67.

51. Ibid., no. 58.

52. Ibid., no. 59.

53. See chap. 7, above.

54. See chap. 6, above.

9. AESTHETICS AND EVANGELICAL
CATHOLICITY IN THE *B MINOR MASS*

1. See Pierre Barbaud, *Haydn*, trans. Kathrine Sorley Walker (New York: Grove Press, 1959), 32.

2. Quoted in Einstein, *Mozart*, 319.

3. Etienne Gilson, *The Arts of the Beautiful* (New York: Charles Scribner's Sons, 1965), 175.

4. Arnold, *Bach*, 82–83.

5. Spitta, *Bach* 3:43–44.

6. Schweitzer, *Bach* 2:314.

7. Luther, *An Order of Mass and Communion*, LW 53:20.

8. Luther, preface to *The German Mass*, LW 53:63.

9. Walter Blankenburg, *Einführung in Bachs h-moll Messe*, 3d ed. (Kassel, 1974), 14.

10. See chap. 7, above.

11. Sven-Erik Brodd, *Evangelisk Katolicitet* (Lund, 1982), 104–135 on Söderblom; see 277–81 on my own (as Brodd terms it) "dialectical" use of the concept.

12. Karsten Harries, *The Bavarian Rococo Church: Between Faith and Aestheticism* (New Haven: Yale University Press, 1983), 1–9.

13. André Pirro, *L'esthétique de Jean-Sebastien Bach* (Paris, 1907).

14. Moritz von Engelhardt, *Valentin Ernst Loescher nach seinem Leben und Wirken*, 2d ed. (Stuttgart, 1856), 25.

15. On these, see chap. 1, above.

16. See chap. 2, above.

17. Spitta, *Bach* 3:77.

18. Quoted in Schweitzer, *Bach* 2:16.

19. See chap. 3, above.

20. I have examined some of these issues in *The Christian Tradition* 2:91–145.

21. See the quotation from Schweitzer in chap. 4, above.

22. Friedrich Smend, "Bachs h-moll-Messe: Entstehung, Überlieferung, Bedeutung," *BJb* 34 (1937):51–57.

23. Pelikan, *Christian Tradition* 2:183–98.

24. Christianus Democritus, *Anfang, Mittel und Ende der Ortho- und Heterodoxie* (n.p., 1699), 67.

25. Schweitzer, *Bach* 2:317–18.

26. Albert Schweitzer, *The Quest of the Historical Jesus*, trans. William Montgomery (1956; New York: Macmillan Co., 1961), 3.

27. John Calvin, "Adversus Petri Caroli calumnias," *Corpus Reformatorum* (Berlin and Leipzig, 1834–), 7:316.

28. Schweitzer, *Bach* 2:319.

29. Helmuth Rilling, *Johann Sebastian Bach's B-Minor Mass*, trans. Gordon Paine (Princeton: Prestige Publications, 1984), 17.

30. Schweitzer, *Bach* 2:315.
31. See chap. 8, above.
32. Schweitzer, *Bach* 2:323.

10. JOHANN SEBASTIAN BACH—
BETWEEN SACRED AND SECULAR

1. Leo Schrade, "Bach: The Conflict Between the Sacred and the Secular," *Journal of the History of Ideas* 7 (1946):151–94.
2. David-Mendel, *Bach Reader,* 24; italics added.
3. See chaps. 2 to 5, above.
4. David-Mendel, *Bach Reader,* 422.
5. Alfred Dürr, *Zur Chronologie der Leipziger Vokalwerke J. S. Bachs* (Kassel, 1976).
6. Ibid., 120.
7. Friedrich Blume, "Outlines of a New Picture of Bach," *Music and Letters* 44 (1963):214–27.
8. Reprinted as Gerhard Herz, "Toward a New Image of Bach," *Essays on J. S. Bach,* ed. George Buelow (Ann Arbor, Mich.: UMI Research Press, 1985), 149–84.
9. Wolff, *Bach Family,* 96–97.
10. John Ogasapian, "Bach: The 'Fifth Evangelist'?" *Journal of Church Music* (March 1985).
11. Martin J. Naumann, "Bach the Preacher," in *The Little Bach Book,* ed. Theodore Hoelty-Nickel (Valparaiso, Ind.: Valparaiso University Press, 1950), 14–15.
12. See chap. 8, above.
13. Naumann, "Bach the Preacher," 18.
14. William K. Wimsatt, Jr., "The Intentional Fallacy," *The Verbal Icon: Studies in the Meaning of Poetry* (1954; New York: Noonday Press, 1966), 3–18.
15. See chap. 1, above.
16. Bruno Walter, *Gustav Mahler,* trans. Lotte Walter Lindt (New York: Alfred A. Knopf, 1958), 108–9.
17. Arnold, *Bach,* 55.
18. Wolff, *Bach Family,* 124.
19. Spitta, *Bach* 2:622.
20. Wolff, *Bach Family,* 107.
21. See chap. 5, above.
22. Arnold Schering, "Über Bachs Parodieverfahren," *BJb* 18 (1921):49.
23. See chap. 2, above.
24. See chaps. 6 and 8, above.
25. See chap. 2, above.
26. See chap. 9, above.
27. Arnold, *Bach,* 4.
28. David-Mendel, *Bach Reader,* 58–60.

29. David-Mendel, *Bach Reader,* 316.
30. See chap. 8, above.
31. See chap. 9, above.
32. Spitta, *Bach* 3:80–81.
33. See David-Mendel, *Bach Reader,* 459.
34. Arnold, *Bach,* 95.

Index

1. CONTEMPORARIES OF BACH

INDEX

2. WORKS OF BACH

Howard